COMING OF AGE
AT THE MILLENNIUM

COMING OF AGE
AT THE MILLENNIUM

*Embracing the Oneness
of Humankind*

by

Nathan Rutstein

Starr Commonwealth
Albion, Michigan

Starr Commonwealth, 13725 Starr Commonwealth Road, Albion MI 49224
Copyright © 1999 by Nathan Rutstein
Printed in the United States of America

05 04 03 02 01 00 99   5 4 3 2 1

Design by Patrick J. Falso, Allegro Design Inc.

ISBN 0-9672577-0-0

CONTENTS

PREFACE

I have felt for a long time that a book on the oneness of humankind was needed. If there were a book that explained with clarity why it is important for individuals and their communities to internalize this reality, I felt, it would help the effort to make our world a more peaceful place. If we were all to believe that we are related, there would be less feuding, suspicion, fighting, and racism. We would discover a natural desire to get along better.

I have discovered over the years that when most people are asked if they are aware of the principle of the oneness of humankind, they usually say they have heard of it, but further probing reveals that they are unaware of the realities underlying the principle. Their understanding is, at best, superficial. To them, "the oneness of humankind" sounds right and good, and, therefore, they won't denounce it. In fact, they may even celebrate it in a house of worship from time to time, but for the most part they don't really think about it. Perhaps deep down they feel the oneness of humankind is a pipe dream. As a consequence, they continue living in a divided society, often carrying deep allegiances to their particular group, which usually leads to the development of antisocial feelings of prejudice.

It is time for us to devote serious time and thought to internalizing this reality, which has always existed. It is imperative that we do it, especially at a time when the Earth's population is swelling and technological advances are bringing us face to face with people we may only have read about a few years ago but never dreamed of meeting. By embracing the principle of oneness, our interactions with those who seem "different" will most likely lead to genuine and friendly relationships. As a rule, family members have a tendency to want to get along with one another.

Initially, one book is not likely to make much of an impact in opening up people's eyes to a long-standing reality such as the oneness of human-kind. Then why the effort in writing the book? Because every spark is a potential fire.

Truthfully, I didn't feel qualified to write the book. Over a ten-year pe-riod I asked a number of people to write it. At times I pleaded for them to take on the challenge. These good people had many compelling reasons as to why they couldn't take on such a project. So with great trepidation I launched into writing something I wasn't sure would ever turn into a pub-lished book.

It has been an incredible learning experience. I never realized just how intimately related all six billion human beings are genetically and spiritu-ally, or just how important it is to help as many people as possible to under-stand and internalize our oneness. Knowing what I now know, I can see things I couldn't see before. I now know why it is humanity's destiny to finally recognize its oneness and unite as one family.

If the voice of this book resembles that of a teacher, it is no accident. During twenty-two years as a professional teacher, I developed the habit of relying on passion and repetition to communicate important points. I know that literary critics often frown upon repetition. But this book was not writ-ten to impress them. I have learned through experience in the college classroom that freeing people from their emotional attachments to false beliefs requires repetition.

I do this with a sincere desire to help readers—my brothers and sisters—overcome whatever holds them back from experiencing real freedom from prejudice. To achieve this delicate goal, I expose readers to historical and scientific information that may, at first glance, be offensive. It will seem to contradict what they have been led to believe by well-meaning teachers and even clerics. Most of us subscribe to the biblical verse, "The truth shall make you free." At times, however, the truth is difficult to accept, especially when it contradicts deeply held beliefs. I know what that is like: It was difficult for me to accept what I had unearthed as I researched the book. It was difficult because I had placed so much faith in certain beliefs that I discovered were unfounded. I learned things about my own country in relation to the treatment of its minorities that I found disturbing. What I discovered didn't diminish my love for my country. I did realize, however, that while there is much about it that is good, it isn't perfect. It has shortcomings. I can honestly say that, through my exploration of the truth about the development of America and through my exploration of the oneness of humankind, I have become a more enlightened citizen who sincerely desires to help his country reach its great destiny.

This book is an attempt to explain why it is important for everyone to recognize and internalize the principle of the oneness of humankind and to explain how such knowledge can benefit both the individual and the community, as well as humanity in general. In the process, the nature of racism—a major obstacle to embracing the oneness of humankind—is explored. The myths that have long bolstered the prevailing view that humanity is composed of different families that are not meant to come together is identified and exposed. As a consequence, readers will become aware of the many realities underlying the principle of the oneness of humankind. They will learn that all humans are endowed with the capacity to unite with others, regardless of ethnicity, culture, religion, or skin color. They will learn about the scientific evidence that proves all humans are related.

Spiritual proofs of the oneness of humanity are also provided. By the end of the book, readers will gain a better understanding of the term "children of God." Those proofs are based on some assumptions. I believe there is a Creator of our universe, Who is always ready to assist sincere seekers of His guidance. However, God's guidance doesn't stop there. In unfathomable ways, He draws humanity closer to its destiny, which is its unification. The basic mechanics by which this is being done remain a mystery. Though God is an unknowable essence, we get to know Him through the likes of an Abraham, Moses, Krishna, Jesus, Buddha, Muhammad, Bahá'u'lláh. These divinely chosen extraordinary figures not only reflect the attributes of God but serve as channels through which God's spiritual and social guidance flows to humankind. Evolutionary in nature, this guidance suits the needs of those to whom the divine messengers are sent. It is reassuring to me to know that our Supreme Parent's love of His children is constant. To receive it, however, one must seek it.

Near the end of the book, I dare to share a dream: I describe my concept of what the world will look like when humanity finally recognizes and embraces the reality of the oneness of humankind.

Writing this book has been a journey to the source of brilliant light. My hope is that the reader will find the path to the same source.

—NATHAN RUTSTEIN, 1999

CHAPTER 1

A CHILD'S PAINFUL DISCOVERY

Sam thought it would never happen to him. That is, being personally stressed over skin color. Normally, those of European extraction don't have to worry about such things in America, where Whites are in political, economic, and social control, and minorities are still trying to unravel themselves from the White-woven web of institutionalized racial prejudice.

If four of his grandchildren were to live in America, they would automatically be ensnared in that web and would face a struggle they aren't prepared for. Just thinking about what they would have to endure, should they move to America, disturbs Sam. Though he wishes he could see them more often, he feels relieved whenever he recalls where they have lived since their birth: in countries where skin color is not a concern. At this point in their development they are pure-hearted, innocent, and bright youngsters, free of the paralysis of internalized racism. They have a healthy sense of themselves, never having had to choose whether to live in a Black or White world. The only world they know is the human world. They are fortunate because their parents have internalized the principle of the oneness of humankind and associate, for the most part, with people who share the same beliefs.

But there are times when Sam's grandson and three granddaughters come to America to visit their grandparents, uncles, aunts, and cousins. When that happens Sam is seized by two clashing emotions: on the one hand, there is happiness for obvious reasons, and on the other hand, fear. Sam is afraid that his grandchildren from overseas will be confronted by the monster of racism. He doesn't want them to lose their self-respect, their sense of nobility, their fundamental goodness, their joy for life, and have to fight the doubts about their humanness that they would undoubtedly pick up should they live in America for some time. He doesn't want them to feel that their brown skin makes them inferior to those of a lighter hue.

What Sam feared would happen did happen in the most unlikely place— in his own kitchen. He and his grandson were seated at the table, facing the deck outside. The youngster, who was only four at the time, was focused on the squirrels dashing about, hunting for scraps of food. Apparently, there were no squirrels in the country where he lives. He was absolutely fascinated with what was unfolding before him. As a gloating grandfather, Sam was impressed with his grandson's power of concentration, his high-spirited curiosity. Sam began to fantasize: "The child has the makings of an outstanding biologist." He was envisioning a day when the boy would be awarded a Ph.D. and would make breakthroughs in research.

Sam's exalted state of being was suddenly shattered when his grandson turned to him and said, while running a finger up his arm, "Grandpa, why do you have a different color than me?"

Sam had not expected that kind of question from his four-year-old grand-child. So young, he thought, and already showing concern about race. But that wasn't the only reason the boy's question hurt him. The question seemed to imply that perhaps the boy didn't belong in Sam's family. That thought was a dagger thrust into his heart. Sam wanted to hug his grandson and assure him that he was a very important part of the family. Instead, the old man closed his eyes and tried hard not to cry. Not speaking helped him to keep from crying. After what seemed to be the longest minute of Sam's life, the child asked, "Is there anything wrong Grandpa?"

Sam lied. "Oh no," he said, fearful of sharing his true feelings.

Aware that he had to answer the child's original question, Sam took hold of his little brown hand and shared with him what he felt at the time was an answer to a prayer: "You see, people are made up of different colors because God loves variety as well as unity. Take, for example, a flower garden. A garden with only brown or white flowers is not as beautiful as a garden with yellow, purple, red, orange, pink, black, and white flowers."

There was no response from his grandson then, nor ever since, and Sam was left wondering if the child got the message. Though Sam would like to ask him if he understood, he shies away from asking because it would only lead to confronting aspects of racism that the boy is still too young to grasp. Not that Sam's grandson hasn't already felt the sting of racism. There have been other trips to Grandpa and Grandma's house since the day their grand-son posed the question that was so difficult to answer.

At a family reunion at Sam's home in the summer of 1998, the child came face to face with the monster of racism. It wasn't on his grandfather's premises. The boy and seven of his cousins, who would be considered White in our skin-color-conscious society, decided to venture out into the neigh-borhood. It wasn't long before the youngster came running home in tears.

He had been called a "nigger" by a group of local children playing kick ball. While he had never heard the term before, he sensed the derisive and hostile spirit in which the word had been spoken. He knew he had been ridiculed. It didn't matter that his "White" cousins had come to his defense. He had been made to feel different in an inferior sense. It was a new experience, Sam feared, that the child would never forget—one that would raise all sorts of doubts about himself, doubts that would most likely stay with him throughout adulthood and could well evolve into a painful identity struggle.

Sam's son and daughter-in-law, whose father is of African descent, were upset. Sam was fuming, not only because of the incident, but because there was nothing he could do to heal the wound. Telling his eight-year-old grandchild that the kids who had accosted him with a racial slur were ignorant and foolish wasn't going to relieve his pain. Nor would an explanation of the nature of prejudice or a discourse on the realities underlying the principle of the oneness of humankind. It was the child's heart that needed to be addressed, not his mind. All Sam could do was hug him and tell him how much he loved him.

Because of that incident, Sam discovered something about himself that he had not been aware of. Though he had never considered himself a violent person, Sam realized he honestly didn't know whether he would be able to control himself if he were to hear someone call his grandson and three granddaughters "niggers."

A FRACTURED VIEW OF HUMANITY

Having to deal with his grandson's introduction to racism was tough on Sam, not only because of the pain it has generated in the boy, his parents, and grandparents. Sam's also bothered by the fact that so many people have been infected by this community-crippling disease and, because of it, are unable to recognize and take to heart the oneness of humankind. Furthermore, knowing that internalizing this reality is a healing balm and that so few have experienced it saddens Sam.

Defining Racism

Racism, which has caused untold suffering through the ages, is a distorted view of reality based on falsehoods that are believed to be facts. White, Asian, and Black supremacist beliefs are actually a set of irrational, fixed ideas and feelings that are hard to control. A person who is driven by conscious or subconscious racist views is being governed by an obsession—an obsession that comes into play whenever he or she engages in an interracial encounter. In essence, racial prejudice is an unquestioned emotional attachment to a falsehood that is assumed to be the truth—in effect, an emotional commitment to ignorance. Sadly, this condition afflicts most people in the world, including many who are highly educated, even people of goodwill who want to do the right thing in their relationships. Because racial prejudice is part of the collective consciousness of, for example, North America, and a powerful element in the Canadian and American cultures, even people who don't choose to harbor negative racial feelings develop them simply by living in a country founded and governed by men who truly believed that those who weren't White were inherently inferior. Racial attitudes were formed and evolved into acceptable, deeply entrenched norms.

North American Racism—The Forging of an Obsession

A classic example of how this irrational, fixed idea and set of feelings called racism develops can be seen in the way America's European settlers treated those who were not White and in how their twisted behavioral pattern influenced their government's treatment of people of color. The following brief historical overview will show how this racial obsession was forged, how a nation conceived as a bastion of freedom became fundamentally racist. The founders of the nation were not evil men; they simply had a warped view of race, as did their followers. One reinforced the other, producing a social miscarriage of justice that is only beginning to be corrected.

The Native Americans

As far as we know, in 1400 A.D. no European colonies existed in what is today known as North America. It is doubtful that any Whites at all were present. But there were between nine and twelve million human beings living on the continent, and their ancestors had lived there for thousands of years. To these people, the idea of calling their continent "the new world" was preposterous.

Just as Europe included nations such as France, Holland, Spain, Portugal, and England, North America was comprised of nations of indigenous people such as the Navajo, the Cherokee, the Mohawk, the Cree, the Choctaw, and many others. Approximately 120 different languages were spoken, and each nation had its own distinct culture. The inhabitants of each nation did not share identical physical characteristics. They did, however, share a similar religion; however, like the many sects of Christianity, they did not all observe the same rites and traditions. Theirs was a pantheistic religion; they believed that God was reflected in all of creation—in rocks, plants, animals, and humans.

In general, the American Indians were a spiritually centered people with a great reverence for life and a deep appreciation for humanity's place within the balance of nature. Many Indian nations observed a strict moral code. Their languages did not have a word for "lie" or "lying." Why? Because lying was an absolutely foreign practice. It simply wasn't done. Their word was their bond. When European settlers during the Colonial period broke a treaty with an Indian nation, the Indians found such behavior barbaric, inhuman. The Founding Fathers continued the pattern of breaking treaties with American Indians, as did those who took over the reigns of power. By the late 1800s, the U.S. government had signed more than four hundred treaties with the American Indians and violated every single one of them.[1] Materialism was not a problem among most of the Indians, because giving was more natural than taking. Their continent was not the uncivilized wilderness the first White settlers claimed it was. Over the centuries there had been many different civilizations in the Americas, making crucial contributions to the development of humankind in the fields of medicine, mathematics, agriculture, ecology, civil engineering, pharmacology, and architecture. One Indian nation's form of governance influenced the shaping of the government of the United States of America and its democratic institutions. (A more detailed description of Indian contributions to civilization is made later in the book.) This is not to say that the Indians were perfect people. Like their European counterparts, they had shortcomings. Through the years there were wars between various Indian nations, just as there were wars between European nations. The point is that the Indians were civilized human beings, not the savages and pagans the European settlers generally thought they were.

The suffering the American Indians endured at the hands of the early European settlers, and later the American government, took its toll. One can safely state that the American Indians were the target of a genocidal campaign. While most ethnic groups in America have grown in size, the number of American Indians has decreased from an estimated nine to twelve million in the early 1500s to about 350,000 in 1960.[2] Most of the American Indians were bewildered and often shocked by the expansion-minded White men's attitudes and behavior. Chief Black Hawk, the Indian chief who led the Sauk and the Fox Indians in the losing effort to prevent federal troops from driving them out of Illinois, seemed to sum up his people's feelings about White people in his surrender speech, given shortly after raising a white flag, which federal troops ignored, proceeding to massacre women and children as well as warriors:

I fought hard. But your guns were well aimed. The bullets flew like birds in the air, and whizzed by our ears like the wind through the trees in the winter. My warriors fell around me. . . . The sun rose dim on us in the morning, and at night it sunk in a dark cloud, and looked like a ball of fire. That was the last sun that shone on Black Hawk. . . . He is now a prisoner to the white men. He has done nothing for which an Indian ought to be ashamed. He has fought for his countrymen, the squaws and papooses, against white men, who came year after year, to cheat them and take away their lands. You know the cause of our making war. It is known to all white men. They ought to be ashamed of it. Indians are not deceitful. The white men speak bad of the Indian and look at him spitefully. But the Indian does not tell lies. Indians do not steal.

An Indian who is as bad as the white men could not live in our nation; he would be put to death and eaten up by the wolves. The white men are bad schoolmasters; they carry false books, and deal in false actions; they smile in the face of the poor Indian to cheat him; they shake them by the hand to gain their confidence, to make them drunk, to deceive them, and ruin our wives. We told them to leave us alone, and keep away from us; they followed on, and beset our paths, and they coiled themselves among us, like the snake. They poisoned us by their touch. We were not safe. We lived in danger. We were becoming like them, hypocrites and liars, adulterous lazy drones, all talkers and no workers. . . .

The white men do not scalp the head; but they do worse—they poison the heart. . . . Farewell my nation. . . . Farewell to Black Hawk.[3]

Today's White Americans have inherited a psychological obsession that began forming when the first European settlers arrived on the American continent. Their intellectual, emotional, and spiritual reaction to the Indians who greeted them, and to the Africans they enslaved, make up the core of the obsession. Their reaction to the Indians and Blacks was based on ignorance and fear. Quick judgments were made. Had they taken the time to inquire of the dark-skinned Indians and Blacks themselves about their cultures, they most likely would have had a more positive reaction. Perhaps they would have seen that beneath the surface they had much in common. Instead, the European settlers saw a people who dressed differently, ate different kinds of foods, worshipped God differently, lived in "strange" dwellings, and socialized differently. All of this and more represented emotional barriers for the settlers, barriers they couldn't overcome. Because of these barriers, the settlers were unable to embrace the reality that Blacks and Indians—like the Europeans—were their own relatives, all children of God. It was not uncommon for many White settlers to openly proclaim that Indians and Blacks were agents of Satan.

To understand how early White settlers thought of Blacks and Indians, it is helpful to know the views of the leaders who influenced most of the people's thinking.

Influential Leaders of Thought

Among those who greatly influenced the European settlers' attitudes and behavior toward Indians and Africans was Pope Nicholas V, who believed that Black people did not have souls. In 1452 he issued a papal bull entitled Romanus Pontifex, which decreed that Portugal's King Alfonso had the right to "invade, search out, capture, vanquish and subdue all Saracens and pagans whatsoever and all of the land and possessions of these heathens be taken away and reduced to perpetual slavery."[4] This decree was viewed by some European entrepreneurs as a license to engage in the slave trade. It also empowered the Roman Catholic clergy in the Americas to enslave Indians and become involved in the Black slave trade as a means of funding the church's work in the so-called "new world."

No doubt, the English settlers' attitudes toward Indians and Africans was also influenced by Britain's King Henry VII, who issued a decree in 1496 to explorer John Cabot to, "conquer, occupy and possess the lands of heathens and infidels."[5] Reinforcing King Henry VII's view was Queen Elizabeth's open aversion toward Africans, whom the White English people commonly referred to as "Black Moors." Thousands of Blacks lived in England in the mid-1500s, and not all of them were servants. A good number owned property, paid taxes, and participated in local churches. Some held professional positions. While the Queen's attempt to rid England of all Blacks failed, she helped to shape the White English person's negative racial attitude that those who emigrated carried with them to America.[6]

When Massachusetts Bay Colony Governor John Winthrop, who was considered the wisest of the Puritans, learned that smallpox, a disease brought to America by Europeans, was sweeping through Indian villages and killing hundreds of Indians, he attributed the epidemic to an act of God. It was God's way, he believed, of removing obstacles to achieving His believers' rightful destiny. Winthrop believed it was his right to conquer and rule the land occupied by the Indians, whom he believed were savages and pagans.

Leading seventeenth-century European thinkers promoted the theory that American Indians were a separate, lower species—that they had not sprung from the biblical Adam and Eve.[7] The Puritan clergy supported this theory. Reverend Cotton Mather thundered in one of his sermons, "We know not when and how these Indians first became inhabitants of the mighty continent, yet we may guess that the Devil decoyed these miserable savages hither, in hope that the gospel of the Lord Jesus Christ would never come to destroy or disturb his absolute empire over them."[8] Mather and his fellow clergymen held the same views toward the kidnapped Africans. The Puritan church's official reason for sanctioning slavery was to "civilize" a savage people who didn't know, as the English did, who God was. In a way, Puritan thinking with regard to Indians and Blacks is reminiscent of Hitler's deranged thinking about Jews. In the end, what the Puritan leadership believed, their followers believed.

A lot of damage was done in the name of God. For nearly two hundred years in Maryland the Jesuits not only kept slaves to work their farms, they also engaged in breeding and trading slaves. The profits were used to further "God's work."[9] In 1731, a leading Baptist evangelist, Dean Berkeley of Rhode Island, refused to give Blacks the sacraments of the church, urging his parishioners to "consider the Blacks as creatures of another species. . . ."[10] "Talk to a planter about the soul of a Negro," commented a writer in a popular colonial journal, "and he's apt to tell you that the body of one Negro may be worth 20 pounds (approximately 40 dollars), but the souls of a hundred of them would not yield him one farthing [a British coin worth about one-sixth of an American cent]."[11] In 1767, several Presbyterian churches in Virginia engaged in a lucrative religious enterprise that started with the purchase of two fertile young slave women. These women were rented out to plantation owners and overseers. By 1835, seventy slave women were being rented out, some as young as thirteen. The White plantation owners were permitted to do whatever they wished with these slave women, including having sex with them. As for the profits? The clergymen used them to supplement their salaries and lived quite well.[12]

According to Historian Fredric Bancroft, "inter-race sexual immorality was one of the worst features of slavery."[13] Many White planters and their White overseers had their favorite slave mistresses. And it didn't matter that a slave woman had a husband. What the master wanted he took. The result

of such sexual encounters between Whites and slaves was offspring classified as "mulatto." The mulatto woman became a highly prized product in
the slave breeding business. White men, slaveholders as well as sexual ad-
venturers from both the North and the South, would pay as much as $5,000
for a mulatto woman. Some of the female slaves who were being sold for
sex were only twelve years old. New Orleans became the leading market for
mulatto slave women.

The sale of mulatto slave women became so popular that poet Henry
Wadsworth Longfellow was moved to write the following lines:

The slaver led her from the door,
He led her by the hand,
To be his slave and paramour
In a strange and distant land![14]

There were clergymen who were not shy about resorting to brutish behavior in disciplining slaves. Reverend Samuel Gray, a Virginian, recovered
a runaway slave and had another slave beat the runaway to death.[15] Flog-
ging of "obstinate" slaves was a common practice. So was the splitting up of
slave families. Slave parents and children were often sold to different White
planters or Northern industrialists. As a result, most of those who were sold
never saw their loved ones again.

From the time the slaves arrived in North America, generation after generation of churchgoers had heard spokesmen of God speak of the inherent
inferiority of Blacks and Indians. And not all of the parishioners were White.
It is very difficult for a religious person not to internalize what is considered
divinely sanctioned. Good, hardworking men, women, and children accepted as truth the preacher's warped view of dark-skinned people—people

who, in reality, were members of the same human family and were all God's children. In those days the principle of the oneness of humankind was virtually unknown. As a consequence, the sincere God-fearing, churchgoing White person living in America in the seventeenth, eighteenth, nineteenth, and early twentieth centuries was unaware of having embraced a concept that generated such suffering and misery among Black and Indian men, women, and children for nearly four hundred years. They did not know they were living a lie.

Many White Christian clergymen—from heads of denominations to rural pastors—endorsed slavery, owned slaves, and engaged in slave trading. In fact, it was a group of White Protestant clergymen who concocted the slave catechism, which was to inculcate in the Black man, woman, and child the belief that they were inherently inferior to Whites, that their purpose in life was to do the bidding of their master, the White man. Every time the slaves assembled for church services, they were required to recite the catechism. The ministers, standing in the pulpit and acting as spokesmen of God, peered down on the slaves, whom God knew were His children. Sadly, the ministers were unaware of this truth. In this religious dialogue, which lasted about fifteen minutes, the slaves were forced to participate in exchanges such as the following:

Pastor: Who keeps the snakes and all bad things from hurting you?
Slaves: God does.
Pastor: Who gave you a master and a mistress?
Slaves: God gave them to me.
Pastor: Who says that you must obey them?
Slaves: God says that I must.

Pastor: What book tells you these things?
Slaves: The Bible.[16]

The catechism included twelve other similar calls and responses. Imagine what it must have been like for the slaves to recite this catechism every time they attended church services. Stripped of their rich cultural heritage, prohibited from learning to read and write, never having experienced freedom, they could do little to ward off the effects of the religious brainwashing administered by the spokesmen of God.

The slave catechism surely must have been a factor in causing what is known as post-traumatic slave disorder—a disorder that continues to plague many African Americans today. Joy Leary, an educational psychologist who claims to suffer from the disorder, reveals one way that this affliction is played out today: Many African-American mothers habitually respond negatively when a White person compliments their children. They may respond with a comment such as "Oh, you don't know how they really are—they're bad." "The reason for the negative response," Leary explains, "is to protect their children from being snatched away. During slavery, slave owners would seize bright slave children from their mother and sell them to other slave owners."[17]

The slave system denied marriages among slaves, separated common-law husbands, wives, and children, and forced Black women to bear White men's children—all contributing to the legacy of today's fragmented Black family life.

The European settlers adopted the racist views of their religious and political leaders. The colonial schools reflected these views, which were passed from grade to grade, from colony to colony, and from generation to generation. By the time the United States of America came into being, a collective educational attitude regarding the status of people of color in the new nation had been set. The attitude reflected the general thinking and feelings of Colonial Americans. Even the Founding Fathers manifested this attitude.

Our Founding Fathers

Benjamin Franklin, perhaps the most sophisticated and enlightened Founding Father, promoted the idea of using rum as a way "to Extirpate these savages [American Indians] in order to make room for the cultivators of the earth."[18] Thomas Jefferson, who drafted the Declaration of Independence, had his runaway slaves flogged and looked upon slave breeding as one would look upon the breeding of dogs or horses. Though in principle he was opposed to the institution of slavery, Jefferson suspected Blacks of being "inferior to the whites in the endowment both of body and mind."[19] Perhaps that's why Jefferson believed Blacks were a form of orangutan and therefore had no place in a country such as the United States of America as citizens.[20] His solution to the Black and White issue was to round up all Blacks and deport them either to Africa or to an island in the Caribbean.[21] Jefferson's views regarding the deportation of African-Americans were also shared by James Madison, who drafted the Bill of Rights, as well as James Monroe, Andrew Jackson, Henry Clay, Daniel Webster, Francis Scott Key, and Abraham Lincoln. Yes, Lincoln! Prior to his election as president of the United States, Lincoln, the "Great Emancipator," declared in a debate with Senator Steven Douglas that Blacks were incapable of functioning effectively in a democracy, and he spoke out against interracial marriage. In one of his speeches in 1858, Lincoln reiterated his feelings about Blacks: " I will say, then, that I am not, nor ever have been, in favor of bringing about in any way the social and political equity of the white and black races [applause]; that I am not, nor ever have been, in favor of making voters or jurors of Negroes, nor qualifying them to hold office, nor to intermarry with white people. . . . And inasmuch as they [the races] cannot so live, while they do remain together there must be a position of superior and inferior, and I, as much as any other man, am in favor of having the superior position assigned to the white race."[22]

America's official view of Blacks just before the Civil War was summed up in the United States Supreme Court's Dred Scott decision. Chief Justice Roger Taney declared that Blacks "are not included, and were not intended to be included, in the word 'citizen' in the Constitution . . . being a subordinate and inferior class of beings."[23] All of those views and more were naturally inculcated in the nation's educational institutions.

It is important to acknowledge that what teachers and textbooks did or did not say about race was only part of what reinforced the White psychological obsession concerning people of color. That White students had no association with Black or Indian children in the classroom from the 1600s to the early1900s sent a message that needed no explanation. Its meaning was clear to all: "Superior" Whites and "inferior" people of color don't mix socially, and that included the school context. At the same time, all students were taught a version of history that made Whites look like heroes while the rest were made to look like uncivilized obstacles to the fulfillment of America's mission. People of color didn't count. Everyone learned, for example, that a Spaniard named Hernando de Soto had been the first person to discover the Mississippi River. All students, including myself, embraced the information as the truth, as did the teachers who shared it. When asked in an exam to name the discoverer of the Mississippi River, I wrote down what my teacher had told me, and my answer was marked correct.

We believed this falsehood as the truth, because of the likes of Winthrop, Mather, Jefferson, Madison, Franklin, and Andrew Jackson, who viewed the Indians living along the Mississippi River as members of a lower order of human beings who could not be considered fully human.

Thus teachers were justified in proclaiming that a European had discovered the Mississippi River. In essence, our teachers taught us that the thousands of Indians who had been living on both sides of the river for thousands of years and using it as a trading artery were not really human. They simply didn't count.

A National Pathology

For more than three centuries, all Americans have been exposed to this type of thinking, leading to the creation of a persistent national pathology. We have been locked into a cycle of blind imitation in which everyone has unwittingly practiced the racial beliefs held by the first White settlers and the Founding Fathers. It has been drilled into us repeatedly from one generation to another. Those heartfelt beliefs, based on a twisted view of reality, have taken such strong hold in the population that not even the abolitionist movement, the Civil War, the end of Jim Crow laws, the civil rights movement, or school busing have been able to change them. What has changed is how those heartfelt beliefs are expressed. Today, Whites are more diplomatic than they were before the 1960s. Two worlds still exist in America. The world of the "superior" Whites and the world of the "inferior" people of color. There is still little genuine mixing in school and church, and interracial friendships based on equality are a rarity.

Unfortunately, those people of goodwill who realize that they hold an attitude of superiority toward people of color have no place to go to overcome it. As a consequence they plunge into denial, which is a carefully concealed mental maneuver springing from a sense of shame. This kind of denial is widespread, and the people of color know it.

When I ponder the harm that has been done and is still being done to countless millions of people over the centuries because of a set of groundless beliefs that have been accepted as the truth, I am overcome by a desire to cry out, "This shouldn't be!" Not only because of the atrocities that have been committed in the name of racial superiority, but because, in reality, humanity is a family. Unfortunately, most of us are not aware of that fact. And if we hear about it, it is dismissed as an abstraction or a distant, idealistic concept that defies practicality.

I could weep when I imagine what the world would be like had ancient humans been aware of, and taken to heart, the reality of the oneness of humankind—and had their descendants embraced it wholeheartedly. I doubt that there would have been an Auschwitz or Buchenwald; Hutus and Tutsis massacring one another; Irish Catholics and Protestants fire-bombing each other's churches; or Serbs, Croatians, and Bosnian Muslims slaughtering each other. The gross human bloodletting of the past would never have happened, and nine million Africans would not have perished during forced voyages to American slavery. Nor would history have recorded the murder of six million Jews in the Holocaust, as well as the death of millions of American Indians who were killed by a government consumed with greed and driven by the warped concept of "Manifest Destiny." The Japanese rape of Nanking would have never happened. I doubt if there would be today the deep-seated suspicion between ethnic groups, the feelings of superiority and inferiority that plague so many men and women. The widespread starvation in the southern Sudan wouldn't exist; nor would the abject poverty that plagues one-quarter of the Earth's population. The kind of hatred, resentment, and jealousy that exists between people today wouldn't exist. What a waste of human energy and resources! What a price to pay in terms of human misery! All because of humanity's ignorance of its oneness, its familyhood.

Not that there wouldn't be any hatred or suspicion in a racial prejudice-free society that's based on a collective understanding of the oneness of humankind. Through the ages those negative emotions have been expressed among brothers and sisters in some nuclear families and will most likely be manifested in the future. But such expression would be the exception rather than the rule. In general, there is among most humans a natural instinct to love and protect their family members, and this instinct is carried out everywhere every day. If the great majority of men, women, and children in the world were to recognize and accept the oneness of the human family and internalize it, they would naturally be protective and loving to everyone on our planet, regardless of geographical location, culture, language, religion, education, or skin color.

So the challenge is for all Earthlings to extend the love we feel for the members of our nuclear family to our greater family—to all of humanity. In doing so, we would be embracing a reality that has existed ever since humans appeared on our planet. Our capacity for compassion and altruism would deepen and broaden. We would view Earth as our common abode, considering all humans our family members, and we would treat each other as such.

Though we are all potentially capable of extending our love for our nuclear family to our greater family, it has not yet happened on a grand scale. Deeply rooted, distorted beliefs about the makeup of humankind must be overcome before such large-scale changes can be made.

Many of these beliefs were fashioned when mountain ranges, seas, even rivers kept different groups of people from interacting regularly. The lack of communication between these people produced prejudices that were incorporated into their cultures. If they did meet, it was often on a battlefield. Those who survived the wars returned home with tales that reinforced the existing prejudices. Those who were captured were usually enslaved, and the feelings of superiority and inferiority between the conqueror and the conquered were heightened. For centuries, most people possessed a fractured view of humanity. Their suspicion and ignorance of other ethnic groups was so deeply rooted that, with the exception of a few enlightened scholars, most people viewed different populations as different species. This is a belief that was more felt than stated. As a consequence, interethnic marriage was felt by many people to be a cardinal sin—in some circles an act of bestiality. While these feelings prevailed prior to the 1300s, there was never any mention of race. The word "race" did not emerge until the height of the European slave trade.

Philosophical Support for Racism

Nevertheless, philosophical giants such as Aristotle espoused the belief in the inherent superiority and inferiority of certain groups of people, legitimizing the racist view in the minds of many people in the past and present. In his *Politics,* this classical Greek thinker who influenced the shaping of future social thought championed slavery. He did not believe in the equality of humankind. Aristotle argued that the slave, by nature, was only a partial human being, lacking a soul, and therefore needed to be ruled by those possessing a soul.[24] The eminent French Philosopher Jean Jacques Rousseau, who had a revolutionary effect on modern political thinking, echoed Aristotle's belief. "Nothing can be more certain," he claimed, "than that every man born in slavery is born for slavery. Slaves lose everything in their chains, even the desire to escape from them; they love servitude. . . ."[25]

Advocates of American slavery used Aristotle and Rousseau's arguments to support their cause, thus contributing to the development of modern racism and the reinforcement of humanity's fractured view of itself. Senator John C. Calhoun of South Carolina, an avid champion of slavery and one of the most erudite lawmakers in Congress before the Civil War, often stated publicly that because ancient Greece, the cradle of Western democracy, condoned and practiced slavery, Americans had every right to own slaves. Calhoun, who called slavery "a positive good,"[26] viewed Blacks as subhuman: "A Negro, being socially, mentally, and anthropologically inferior to a white man, had no rights, deserved none, and could not make responsible use of them."[27] In the early 1800s, during the peak of American slavery, Virginia attorney and editor George Fitzhugh, who possessed a persuasive pen and voice, rationalized the use of slaves, stating, "Men are not born entitled to equal rights. It would be far nearer the truth to say that some were born with saddles on their backs, and others booted and spurred to ride them—and the riding does them good."[28]

"Scientific" Support for Racism

There were other influential contributions to the development of racism and humanity's fractured view of its structure. As late as the 1700s and 1800s, considerable energy and brainpower were generated to uphold the notion that humanity is a hierarchical multiracial creation—that certain "races" were endowed with capacities superior to those of other "races." To prove their point, experts on the human condition propounded various theories regarding the origin and structure of the human species. Differences were stressed. Scientists in crude fashion combed the world, recording the physical and, they believed, spiritual characteristics of different ethnic groups.

They determined, for example, the average size of a group's posterior and compared it with the sizes of other groups' posteriors; the sizes of nostrils were measured, noting the shape of the nose and eyes. Intelligence was determined by the number of lumps of hardened fatty tissue on a head or by the size of one's cranium. Behavior and attitude were also noted. Generation after generation of children and youth accepted falsehoods as the truth. Preferring their own physical and mental characteristics, renowned European thinkers hailed their physical and spiritual attributes as the mark of superiority. Hence these characteristics became the standard for judging beauty, spiritual development, cultural refinement, and intelligence.

The eighteenth-century Swedish biologist Carolus von Linnaeus, who classified thousands of animal and plant species, was one such thinker. Considered the greatest biologist of his day, he undertook to classify humanity. He concluded on the basis of skin color that there were four families of man. His findings became sacrosanct in scholarly circles. What did the distinguished scientist find?

Von Linnaeus described American Indians as reddish, choleric, obstinate, contented, and regulated by customs. He described Europeans as white, fickle, sanguine, blue-eyed, gentle, and governed by laws. Asians were found to be sallow, grave, dignified, avaricious, and ruled by opinions. Africans were categorized as black, phlegmatic, cunning, lazy, lustful, careless, and governed by caprice. Though von Linnaeus had very limited personal contact with three of the four "families of man," his observations and judgments regarding their behavior, personality traits, languages, and moral and intellectual characteristics were embraced by the nineteenth-century fledgling anthropological community, influencing, in turn, the thinking of the larger society. Though von Linnaeus's observations on what would later be termed the races of man were based largely on assumptions and sketchy data related to him by European travelers to Africa, Asia, and the Americas, he became known as the father of anthropology.[29]

About forty years after von Linnaeus set forth his "four families of man" theory, German anatomist and naturalist Johann Freidrich Blumenbach added a fifth family and then redefined all five groups on the basis of geography and appearance, placing the family to which he belonged—the Caucasians—at the he top of the hierarchy of worth (basing this decision, oddly enough, upon perceived beauty and on the belief that Whites looked more like God than any other race) and placing the Africans at the bottom.[30]

The renowned British philosopher David Hume, who had a respectable following among intellectuals, was a committed White supremacist. He proclaimed publicly his sincere belief: "I am apt to suspect the Negroes and in general all other species (for there are four or five different kinds) to be naturally inferior to the whites. There never were a civilized nation of any other complexion than white, nor even any individual eminent either in action or speculation. No ingenious manufacturers among them, no arts, or sciences."[31]

These so-called scientific findings and philosophical pronouncements by prominent European scientists and philosophers fueled the racist American political leadership's belief that Whites were inherently superior to the American Indian and those of African descent. It encouraged some Americans to engage in studies that would support what their European counterparts had discovered. Take, for example, the study organized by the South Carolinian physician Dr. Josiah C. Nott in the 1840s. Nott measured the heads of Blacks and Whites and found that the heads of Black people tended to be smaller than those of White people. From that finding he deduced that Blacks must have smaller brains and must, therefore, be less intelligent than Whites. His views on race, which were later proven to be erroneous, reflected the views of many of his American and European scientific peers in the mid 1800s:

> The brain of the Negro . . . is, according to positive measurements, smaller than the Caucasian by a full tenth; and this deficiency exists particularly in the anterior portion of the brain, which is known to be the seat of the higher facilities. History and observation, both teach that in accordance with this defective organization, the Mongol, the Malay, the Indian and Negro, are now and have been in all ages and all places, inferior to the Caucasian.
>
> There is in the animal kingdom, a regular gradation in the form of the brain, from the Caucasian down to the lowest order of animals . . . the intellectual faculties and instincts are commensurate with the size and form . . . In animals where the senses and sensual faculties predominate, the nerves coming off the brain are large, and we find the nerves of the Negro larger than those of the Caucasian.
>
> No black race . . . has been, or can be established at any great distance from the equator. Look at the bills of mortality . . . and you will see the proportion of death amongst blacks, increasing as you go north, until you go to Boston . . . a cold climate so freezes their brains as to make them insane and idiotical.[32]

Nott's findings were embraced by many intellectuals in the United States as well as in Europe. They inspired the French historian and philosopher Count de Gobineau to write a book entitled *The Inequality of the Human Races,* which became an American bestseller. University biology courses featured Nott's views.[33]

Harvard medical historian Allan Brandt points out that after Nott's revelations, scientists continued to reinforce the White man's warped view of the Black:

By the turn of the century, Darwinism had provided a new rationale for American racism. Essentially primitive peoples, it was argued, could not be assimilated into complex, White civilization. Scientists speculated that in the struggle for survival the Negro in America was doomed. Particularly prone to disease, vice and crime, Black Americans could not be helped by education or philanthropy. Social Darwinists analyzed census data to predict the virtual extinction of the Negro in the twentieth century, for they believed the Negro race in America was in the throes of a degenerative evolutionary process.[34]

Scientific Studies Today

As we approach the twenty-first century, racism remains a major obstacle to world peace. It is understandable why many ethnic groups were suspicious of each other and even hated each other in the past. But now, with the advent of the computer, the communications satellite, television, robotics, the airplane, and free education in most countries, you would think most people would have scrapped their prejudices and embraced the reality of the oneness of humankind. This hasn't happened even though today's scientific community has debunked the myth of multiracialism and has embraced intellectually the reality that there is only one race—the human race—and one human color with many different shades.

Some of the world's leading experts in genetics, anthropology, biology, endocrinology, paleontology, sociology, and social psychology gathered in

Austria in June of 1995 to assess the scientific validity of the concept of race. Summarizing their scholarly discussions, anthropologist Lionel Tiger wrote:

> The fact is that all contemporary population genetics and molecular biology underscores that the nineteenth century notion of races as discrete and different entities is false. There is only gradual genetic diversity between groups. We all merge smoothly into each other. Nearly all the physically observable differences reflect very limited local adaptations to climate and other specific environmental conditions.[35]

Unfortunately, the scientists' proclamation, which was buried in a *Wall Street Journal* article and a few scientific journals, has had a negligible impact. Racism remains rampant despite an increase in tolerance and political correctness among some groups of people. It doesn't seem to matter that in the past fifty years there has been a continuous stream of books, articles, and research exposing the fallacy of racial theories. For example, anthropologist Ashley Montague called race "man's most dangerous myth."[36] Yale University biologist Jonathan Marks wrote, "Race has no basic biological reality."[37] Anthropologist Leonard Leiberman proclaimed that "Misconceptions about race have led to forms of racism that have caused much social, psychological and physical harm. These misconceptions have their origin in various papers and books that depend heavily on old and outmoded biological concepts of race."[38] Anthropologists such as Brown University's John Ladd are bent on setting the record straight: "We the researchers are taking action to correct a legacy of misconception about the biology of race in which earlier generations of researchers provided the raw material for serious claims of racial superiority. They like to concoct a bio-logical basis for mistreating people."[39] According to the American Anthro-pological Association, "differentiating species into biologically defined 'races' has proven meaningless and unscientific as a way of explaining variation, whether in intelligence or other traits."[40]

Most Whites who are aware of the research have resisted emotionally accepting the idea that their ancestral roots are in Africa. It doesn't matter that the *Journal of Science* declared in 1996 that "Most scientists have come to accept the evolutionary theory based on DNA evidence: that modern humans originated in Africa about 270,000 years ago. Researchers at Yale, Harvard and the University of Chicago have traced genetic roots of the human family . . . to the existence of an 'African Eve.'"[41] And it doesn't matter that a popular anthropology text by William A. Haviland states, "All humans appear to have had a 'black (African) ancestry, no matter how 'white' some may be today."[42] The sad fact is that such findings and authori-tative declarations have not moved the great majority of Whites to embrace the truth. They feel more comfortable embracing a falsehood that tradition has drummed into them as the truth.

The same can be said about the majority of Whites' refusal to embrace the principle of the oneness of humankind. This kind of mental and emo-tional resistance prevails among the great majority of people—and Whites are not alone in this resistance—despite the chorus of support for the prin-ciple of the oneness of humankind coming from some of the world's lead-ing scientists. In *The Biology of Race*, Dr. James King reveals, "Since all human beings are of one species and since all populations tend to merge when they exist in contact, group differentiations will be based on cultural behavior and not on genetic differences."[43] Dr. Luigi Luca Cavalli-Sforza, one of the world's leading geneticists, has compiled a definitive atlas of the genetic profiles of over 1,800 population groups around the world. His *History and Geography of Human Genes* is the most comprehensive survey of human genetic variation ever compiled. His conclusion is that there is only one race, the human race.[44] In another book, Cavalli-Sforza states:

> We must remember that what unifies us outweighs what makes us different. Skin color and body shape, language and culture, are all that differentiate the peoples scattered across the earth. This variety, which testifies to our ability to accept change, adapt to new environments and evolve new lifestyles, is the best guarantee of a future for the human race. . . . This diversity, like the changing face of the sea or sky, is minute compared with the infinite legacy we human beings possess in common.[45]

Geneticists estimate that the variations of genetic makeup regarding what is commonly known as racial differences occupy only about one-hundredth of a percent of our genes.[46] The differences are a simple matter of adaptation to one's environment. Our primitive ancestors' genes were programmed to produce dark skin. Their pigment protected them from the tropical sun's ultraviolet rays, which we now know can cause skin cancer. By a flip of the genetic dice, some of the migrants to what we now call Europe had a variant gene that gave them a lighter skin. Because of diet and less disease, these men and women tended to live longer and have more children, who in turn passed the trait on to their descendants. The trend continued for generations, eventually producing fair-skinned northern Europeans.[47] But skin-color change among an ethnic group does not require a supernatural act; it is a natural phenomenon. According to Florida University anthropologist John Moore, "skin-color genes are turned off and on very quickly in evolution. People can go from black to white or white to black in 10,000 years."[48]

According to Harvard biologist Richard Lewontin, the boundary between different "races" is not well defined. No matter how one tries to divide humanity into races, there are always many peoples who do not fit neatly into any of the categories. This is because movement and mixing have always occurred, causing genetic material to pass between widely separated populations.

Though many more scientists shared the same views concerning the oneness of the human family and the falsity of racial theories, destructive beliefs regarding the composition of humanity are intact and continue to keep the human family fractured. While abundant scientific evidence is available, it is not easily accessible for most people, who are not inclined to pick up an academic journal. So far, school systems have failed to teach what modern science has unearthed about the oneness of humankind. In fact, their heavy emphasis on human differences—a recent trend intended to establish social tranquillity in the classroom—has reinforced the popular notion that Germans and Namibians, Indonesians and British, or Blacks and Whites are different races. Aren't schools supposed to expose students to the truth instead of perpetuating proven falsehoods masquerading as the truth?

CHAPTER 3

OVERCOMING THE EMOTIONAL ATTACHMENT TO IGNORANCE

Getting a large number of people to replace their distorted view of humanity with the truth will not be easy. Mere ignorance is not difficult to overcome, for it is easy to train a young child who is pure-hearted and open-minded. It is much more difficult to overcome emotional attachments to falsehoods that are believed to be true.

Americans' Reverence for Columbus

Defusing the emotional attachment to ignorance will require much more effort than overcoming simple ignorance. After all, practically a lifetime of conditioning has gone into developing the emotional attachment.

To illustrate the difficulty of overcoming the emotional attachment to ignorance, take, for example, Americans' reverence for Christopher Columbus, who is hailed as the discoverer of their land. Statues of the explorer dot the American landscape. Cities have been named after him. A federal holiday has been established to honor his birthday. Parades and pageants are held on that day memorializing his exploits. True, the national veneration of Columbus started before the true nature of his exploits in the Western Hemisphere became common knowledge. Today, however, it can certainly be argued that his actions were those of a racist mass murderer. Through Columbus's command, more than 120,000 Arawak Indians were killed, and thousands of others were enslaved and tortured. A popular punishment carried out by Columbus's men was to cut off the hands of those slaves who did not meet their work quota. In 1517, a sympathetic Spaniard, Pedro de Cordoba, wrote in a letter to King Ferdinand,

> As a result of the sufferings and hard labor they endured, the Indians choose and have chosen suicide. Occasionally a hundred have committed mass suicide. The women, exhausted by labor, have shunned conception and childbirth. . . . Many, when pregnant, have taken something to abort and have aborted. Others after delivery have killed their children with their own hands, so as not to leave them in such oppressive slavery.[1]

Though history has recorded the many atrocities Columbus committed when he came to the New World looking for gold, we continue to revere him. We don't want to hear the truth. We don't want to know the truth. We cling tenaciously to the myth of Christopher Columbus, which our hearts have accepted as true. Any attempt to dislodge the myth is vigorously resisted. So we continue to think of a racist mass murderer as the discoverer of America, continue to march in Columbus Day parades, and continue to teach our children the Columbus myth.

It does not seem to matter to us that we are perpetuating a falsehood as the truth. We know the facts, yet we do not allow them to change our feelings about a hero who is known to have committed heinous crimes against his fellow human beings. Let's face it! This is more than strange thinking and behavior, more than a gross injustice. It is a form of an unrecognized insanity. Yes, insanity! The great majority of Americans do not recognize it as such because, for the most part, they all harbor the same feelings about Columbus. The rationalization is, "If others feel the way I do, then what I believe can't be bad. . . . To hell with the facts!"

A more rational and honest reaction to the facts would be to dismantle the statues, rename the cities, and scrap the Columbus Day holiday and all of its associated festivities. But there is no real desire to make the changes. Highly educated adults occupying powerful posts refuse even to consider the idea of change.

Isn't the confusion of fantasy with reality one of the signs of madness? And not only do we confuse fantasy with reality, we revere the fantasy turned reality! Usually, a person who engages in such twisted thinking ends up in a mental hospital.

The Example of Amherst

There are other examples of this madness. The town of Amherst, Massachusetts—arguably one of the most liberal towns in America, a model of political correctness, the site of three colleges, a place where PhDs abound—is named after another racist mass murderer. In fact, one of the town's three colleges is named after him, as are the leading bookstore and the inn that faces the town's handsome green. Until this day, Amherst College's fight song, which hails the character and exploits of the school's namesake, is sung at campus parties and whenever the football team scores a touchdown.

In the mid-1700s Lord Jeffrey Amherst, the commander of British forces in the northern sector of the Crown's North American colonies, gained hero status by helping to win Canada for Great Britain and by engineering a successful ethnic cleansing campaign in New England. He could, perhaps, be considered a pioneer of biological warfare. Amherst hated the American Indians, viewing them as a barrier to human progress—a sentiment shared by most of the colonists. To hasten the elimination of the Indians, Amherst had hundreds of blankets infected with smallpox one winter. Then, in a feigned gesture of goodwill, he invited the American Indians in the Connecticut River Valley to collect the blankets. Hundreds of Indians perished as a result, enabling the European settlers to seize their lands. Recognizing Amherst's "heroic" exploits, the British Crown proclaimed him a lord, and Parliament made him the governor-general of British North America. Later he became the head of the British army.

Today, Lord Amherst's portrait hangs on a wall of the room in which the trustees of Amherst College usually meet. Almost everyone in Amherst is aware of what made Lord Jeffrey Amherst famous, yet no consideration has been given to changing the name of the town, and the college and every other institution named after the infamous general is resistant to making such a change. Paintings of Lord Amherst are still displayed in public places. This, despite most citizens' pro-human rights position and their opposition to nuclear, biological, and chemical warfare, their aversion toward ethnic cleansing, and their advocacy of the peace movement. Somehow the people of Amherst do not seem to recognize that naming a town after Lord

Amherst is like naming a town after Adolph Hitler. The emotional attachment to Lord Amherst's "heroic" exploits remains fixed in most Amhersites' minds. No wonder historian Arnold Toynbee views racial prejudice as irrational: "Our color prejudice has not a shadow of physiological justification but is an instance of an irrational aversion from whatever is different."[2]

Dismantling the Attachment

Despite the difficulty of cracking the emotional attachment to falsehood and ignorance, it can be dismantled. In most cases, a gradual chipping-away process is required.

Exposure to a considerable amount of patience, sustained love, and knowledge are necessary for a person to change beliefs that, through the years, have provided a sense of security and comfort. Challenging one's belief system usually provokes resistance, because there is a desire to protect what makes one feel comfortable and secure. If the challenge is forceful, arguments that lead to fights usually result, and feuds develop. Ideally, the challenge should be laced with love. Truth that is conveyed with sustained and unqualified love can penetrate even the hardest of hearts.

Love is required because those who harbor racial prejudice are still members of our greater human family. To reject them, to belittle them, to treat them as inferior would be a violation in spirit of the principle of the oneness of humankind. Besides, such behavior only intensifies a person's resistance, in turn fueling his or her prejudice. Continued exposure to love will, in most cases, eventually break down even the self-proclaimed bigot's resistance to considering the validity of the oneness of the human family. In time, such an individual will experience a change of attitude that will free him or her from the bondage of bigotry.

A former leader of the Ku Klux Klan had such an experience, thanks to the efforts of a cantor in Lincoln, Nebraska. A few days after moving to Lincoln to serve a small Jewish congregation, the cantor's family received anonymous hate calls, which were soon followed by pamphlets from the local KKK chapter. With the help of a newspaper reporter, the cantor was able to pinpoint the source of the attacks: the head of the Klan in Nebraska. Though the cantor's wife and children tried to dissuade him from calling on the Klansman, he followed his intuition and called on the man who claimed to want to see the cantor and his family dead.

Fear swept over the cantor as he knocked on the Klansman's front door. The stocky, balding man who opened the door to his cluttered apartment was in a wheelchair. A diabetic, he had had both legs amputated. But it wasn't the two stumps that caught the cantor's immediate attention; it was the swastika the Klansman wore around his neck. The pro-Nazi posters on the walls and the guns on the table made the cantor wonder if he were doing the right thing. When he told the Klansman who he was and why he was there, the Klansman erupted. Cursing, he demanded that the cantor leave and reached for a gun. Though the cantor's attempt to initiate a dialogue was summarily rejected, he announced that he would return.

The cantor kept his promise. Though he was rebuffed by the Klansman more than ten times, the Klansman finally broke down and chatted with his sworn enemy. At first, the Klansman would speak for only a few minutes, but gradually a bond began to develop between the two men. They eventually engaged in long philosophical discussions, which led to considerable soul baring by both men. Through these exchanges the two men learned that they had much in common. Both had been abused as children, both had had a run-in with the law as youth, and both had spent time in prison.

During one of these visits, the Klansman suddenly broke into tears and begged for forgiveness. When the cantor later shared with his wife what had happened, she asked to meet the man whom she had feared would blow up her house.

When unfortunate circumstances forced the Klansman to leave his apartment, the cantor, his wife, and children not only helped with the move but also cleaned and painted the Klansman's new apartment.

Eventually, the Klansman resigned from the Klan. Shortly afterward, he began giving a series of talks in Lincoln, stressing the importance of loving all of God's children regardless of skin color, religion, or ethnicity. Many of those who knew the former Klansman felt that his conversion was a miracle. The cantor, however, did not. He recognized that the former Klansman—like all human beings—possessed an unlimited reservoir of love and a constant longing to be loved. He knew that if an individual is not aware of his God-given capacity to love, he will not develop that capacity and will tend to be suspicious and hateful. The cantor, in reaching out to his enemy, simply used what God had endowed him with, and had faith that it would work.

When the former Klansman's diabetes worsened, the cantor and his wife insisted that he move into their home, which was already crowded. Two of the children gave up their bedroom and slept in the basement. While in his friends' home, the former Klansman was literally showered with love. When he was unable to bathe himself, the cantor's wife took care of that responsibility. The children, who were in their late teens and older, often chauffeured him to places where he would give his talks. Their friendship grew into a genuine family relationship.

When the cantor discovered that the former Klansman was not on speaking terms with his parents, he arranged for the parents to come meet with their son. Not long after the tearful reunion, the former Klansman passed away a happy and enlightened man.

Understanding What a Human Being Is

Considering the present condition of the world, it is easy to discount the Klansman's story as exceptional. Though such an occurrence would make the headlines of some newspapers, I doubt that any headway would be made in altering the prevailing fractured view of the structure of humanity that most people hold. Not even a mass conversion of Klansmen would alter the view. In time, this amazing event would be relegated to, at best, a footnote in history, and most people would continue to be ruled by their prejudices. This is because so many people have a distorted understanding of the essential nature of a human being. This misunderstanding is buttressed by centuries-old misconceptions that have become ingrained in human souls and are embraced as the truth.

When people have a true understanding of the essence of a human being, they cannot continue to be racists; nor, for that matter, can they continue simply to be people of goodwill trying to conceal their true negative racial feelings. They are driven by an impulse to view everyone as a family member. Since the great majority of people do not subscribe to such a view, we can only deduce that the great majority of people do not really know what a human being is. They move through life simply reacting to all of the stimuli they encounter, and much of what they encounter is ugly. Consequently, they become slaves to convention, never experiencing true freedom, never truly understanding who they really are.

Why is knowledge of human nature necessary before an individual can discover his or her true self? Without that knowledge, we won't know what to look for—that is, the latent spiritual virtues within us. When these latent virtues are ignored, we allow external forces that are influenced by a dog-eat-dog culture shape our personalities and determine our likes and dislikes.

This lack of understanding of the true nature of a human being became apparent to me while teaching as a college instructor. For eight years, my first assignment in a course entitled "Communicating in Today's World" was as follows: In five hundred words or more, define and describe what a human being is. Not one student, regardless of IQ and Scholastic Aptitude Test scores, had a complete understanding of the reality of a human being. More than 80 percent of the students admitted that they had never pondered the matter before. They simply took their humanness for granted, much as fish take for granted the water in which they live.

Sadly, most secular educational institutions, including universities, do not help students find an answer to the question I posed to my students. In fact, most proceed as if the question were irrelevant. Even students who study anthropology, biology, psychology, or physiology usually graduate with the impression that the human being is fundamentally an animal, albeit Earth's most intelligent animal. The human being's spiritual dimension is not discussed, either because professors give no credence to what they feel are inexplicable issues, or they simply reject it as a fantasy concocted by fearful, wishful-thinking men and women. Though these politically correct-minded academics may never publicly proclaim their belief that spirituality is a synonym for superstition, it is a major factor in shaping their understanding of human nature and the meaning of life. Most of the academics I know believe deep down that life is one big, dangerous jungle and that the human being is our planet's most artful and powerful predator.

Of course, there are religious schools and universities that do not avoid tackling the subject of the nature of man. In fact, such schools try hard to inculcate their religion's teachings on the subject into their students. However, I have observed during twenty-two years as a college instructor, that by teaching that the human being is born in sin, these religious schools set off feelings of fear and anxiety among the students, creating an obstacle to discovering and developing their potentialities. Doubt and confusion set in when the students are exposed to secular views of the nature of man. As a result, more and more students at church-affiliated schools are openly questioning the idea that they and everyone else are born sinners.

The clash between the humanistic view and the traditional Christian view of the reality of man has caused so much confusion and ill will among people that most avoid talking about it. Besides, arguments between liberals and conservatives on this issue are usually based on misconceptions that both sides believe are the truth. Tired of such encounters, many men and women adopt a "plague on all your houses" attitude. When the question of the essence of humanity is raised, most people try to change the subject or psychologically withdraw from the conversation. They become adept at turning to safer subjects such as the weather, sports, music, favorite books, TV shows, or job experiences.

As a consequence, the great majority of people go about their business every day, ignorant of what and who they really are. Without an awareness of the essential nature of man, most people tend to focus on the superficial differences and not the basic similarities between people. Unfortunately, this kind of thinking reinforces the heartfelt sense that Italians, Irish, Blacks, and Whites, for example, are different species. If they believe in God, they have convinced themselves that the different ethnic groups were meant to be distinct and separate, that they are part of God's grand design. Emotionally, they reject references to humanity as the children of God, treating the expression as a meaningless platitude that can find no place in their hearts. If they hear it expressed in a house of worship, they do not take it home with them. And it does not matter that the founders of their religion taught that all the people in the world are members of the same human family. Over the years, converts to their religion have brought fears and suspicions, which have influenced the development of the teachings of their church. Manmade traditions and dogmas have resulted, fostering separation instead of unity.

Take, for example, Christianity: There is the conflict between Protestants and Catholics, played out gruesomely in Ireland for decades. Within Protestantism there is disunity and suspicion between the many denominations. Mainstream Protestants want little to do with Mormons, Jehovah's Witnesses, and Seventh-Day Adventists. In fact, many feel that these relatively new denominations do not even belong in the Protestant category. Pentecostals want nothing to do with mainline Protestant churches, and vice versa. Northern Baptists and Southern Baptists are in theological conflict. The Greek Orthodox and Armenian Churches promulgate cultural separatism as well as their particular interpretations of the teachings of Jesus Christ. According to the first edition of *The World Christian Encyclopedia,* there are 20,780 sects of Christianity in 1982, most of them bastions of exclusivity. All of this has contributed to most people's belief that separatism, not unity, is the will of God. And, for the most part, most people behave accordingly.[3]

This differentiated view of the structure of humanity is a breeding ground for racial, cultural, and ethnic prejudice. Without a true understanding of the nature of a human being, excessive pride in one's ethnicity leads, in time, to feelings of superiority toward other groups of people and eventually evolves into full-blown prejudice. To uphold the sense of superiority, attempts are made to preserve the "purity" of the group. To prevent the "mongrelization" of their people, they discourage serious interactions with other groups, frowning upon interracial or intercultural marriage and encouraging inbreeding. A certain lifestyle that is unique to the group emerges. Indoctrination classes for the group's children are organized. Literature, humor, dance, folklore (which often includes derogatory jokes about other cultures), are developed to help keep the faithful focused on their culture and to guard against their being lured away by alien cultures. Considerable effort is put forth to find scientific support for what is fervently believed to be the truth concerning their position on the composition of humanity.

With a true understanding of the essential nature of a human being, however, people will gain a true understanding of the term "children of God." They will view every human being, regardless of looks, education, religion, gender, language, dress, profession, vocation, or culture, as their family member. They will know that they are endowed with a limitless reservoir of love and will know how to tap it and express it to everyone they meet. They will become living examples of highly developed spiritual beings and will be an inspiration to others.

Unfortunately, when many contemporary learned men and women attempt to explain the reality of man, much effort is put forth to trace the various stages of humanity's biological and social development. The australopithecine, Homo habilis, Homo erectus, and Homo sapiens stages are described, stressing the shape of skulls, spinal columns, the size of brains and jaws. They try to point out who in the past were the plant eaters and the meat eaters and the first tool makers. An educated guess is usually offered as to when apes and humans are supposed to have parted ways in their evolutionary course.

Spiritual Beings Having a Human Experience

The late philosopher and paleontologist Pierre Teilhard de Chardin clarified for many of us what we are when he stated, "We are not human beings having a spiritual experience, we are spiritual beings having a human experience."[4] In other words, we are a soul with a body, and not a body with a soul. The distinction is significant. The body, which is our animal side, is here today and gone tomorrow, subject to the laws of composition and decomposition; but the soul, which is our true reality, is everlasting.

Having said this, it is important to note that the body is not to be neglected. It is an important part of the human makeup. Without it, we would not be able to carry out in our everyday existence the good intentions that spring from the soul.

The soul has a number of distinctive capacities, among them being the capacity to understand, or the "mind"; the capacity to feel, or the "heart"; and the capacity to generate intentions and implement them, or "will." These capacities are used daily, for example, when ideas stem from the soul's capacity to understand. The happiness that the ideas bring us springs from the soul's capacity to feel, and our intention to implement the ideas comes from the soul's capacity to generate intentions and initiate actions.

Of all forms of life, only human beings have the capacity to understand that the planet on which we live is so tiny that it is physically insignificant relative to the rest of the universe. The seal and the falcon are unaware of the universe and of our planet's size, place, and function within it. While animals sense the physical world around them, only human beings are aware of their own consciousness; and unlike animals, humans have the potential to know that other human beings are living in different regions of the world. Monkeys in India, however, aren't aware of the monkeys in Africa or South America. Humanity's uniqueness is reflected in the dynamic configuration of physical and spiritual aspects in our nature, which has the potential for harmony. The nature of this configuration requires continuous development if we are to function as complete human beings. By "complete" I do not mean perfect but, rather, balanced—making steady progress in both spiritual and physical development.

Physically, humans, in some respects, are no match for animals. On a one-to-one basis and unarmed, we do not have the ability to vanquish the tiger or the shark in their respective environments. We do not possess the strength of a gorilla or an elephant. We cannot fly. Yet humans can create an airplane and fly faster, higher, and longer than an eagle; they can build a submarine and explore more of the ocean floor than a shark can. While an elephant can crush a village hut, humans can construct skyscrapers and demolish them with manmade dynamite.

While most animals possess a brain, the human brain is unique. One of its distinguishing characteristics is its cerebral cortex, which processes thought, speech, and memory. Without it, we humans would not be able to create airplanes, submarines, or skyscrapers, nor would we be able to explore outer space, let alone discover the solar system within an atom.

Contrary to popular belief, the human brain is not the same thing as the mind. The brain is simply the organ in the human body that functions as the central control mechanism. It receives, stores, and transmits messages from the mind, which is an aspect of the soul. In other words, a damaged brain is unable to reflect the full scope of the mind, much like a faulty lamp transmits a flickering light.

Built into the physical aspect of our human nature, which includes the brain, are two important instincts that are necessary for humanity's existence. Without the drive for sex and for survival, humanity would become extinct. These drives are natural to us because we are part animal. However, the difference between humans and apes (which are entirely animal), is that apes lack a soul and are completely governed by physical instincts, which are generally regulated by nature.

Because humans are not completely regulated by physical instincts and possess free will, which is an element of the soul, we can reject or ignore our spiritual side and can allow ourselves to become obsessed with sex and survival. When enough people in a community are functioning on that level, the community becomes dysfunctional, very much like present-day America and Europe. A reliable reflection of the societal condition in the West is American and European television, whose major emphasis is sex and survival.

If not regulated by the soul, other human instincts can cause considerable damage. Take anger and greed for example. A spiritually underdeveloped person who becomes angry might wound or kill someone or might become a tyrant, while a spiritually developing person will channel his anger in fighting corruption and injustice. A spiritually underdeveloped person is most likely to exploit, even hurt, others in the pursuit of material wealth, while the spiritually developing person will direct his greed toward acquiring virtues and knowledge.

The Nature of the Soul

Most religious traditions believe that the soul comes into being at the point of conception. While it has a beginning, it has no end. Unlike the body, it is an intangible single spiritual entity—an unknowable essence—that is not subject to the laws of composition and decomposition. It is indestructible. The soul is not inside the body; nor is it attached to it. In a sense, the association of the soul with the body is much like that of a light focused on a mirror. The light cannot be pulled out of the mirror; it is neither inside the mirror nor attached to it. Should the mirror fall and break, the light continues to shine.

The soul is a spiritual emanation of God. There is a connection between the human soul and our Creator, which is a life-creating, life-sustaining, unknowable essence; a connection that can be likened to the relationship between the sun and its rays. When humans ignore or reject their souls, they ignore or reject their connection with God, which is a constant source of love and knowledge. When they choose not to acknowledge this source, they are forced to rely on instincts and are prone to behave in what society condemns as "evil ways." Ignorance, rejection, or a distorted understanding of the divine source by a large number of people can lead to serious troubles among individuals and communities.

Dreaming is a sign of our soul. When we sleep, we are closer to death than in any other human condition. While the soul does not possess ears, a nose, a tongue, legs, or eyes, in our dreams we converse, smell odors, run, touch others, meet people we have never met before, see things we have never seen before, and travel to places we have never been to before. Some of our dreams have a profound impact on us, especially those that were recorded days or years earlier and are recalled when we find ourselves for the first time in the place we had dreamt about meeting people who were in our dream and who change our lives.

An American couple revealed such an experience on national television. The wife, who wanted to have another child but couldn't conceive one naturally, had a vivid dream of a light-skinned woman giving birth to a black-haired, olive-skinned boy. When she awoke, she glanced at her calendar and clock and made note of the day and time: March 8, 2:59 A.M.

Shortly after the woman shared the dream with her husband, the couple received a call from an adoption agency stating that it had found an infant boy for them. When the wife saw the baby, she gasped because it was the same child she had seen being born in her dream.

"What day was the child born?" she asked.

"March 8th," said the social worker.

"And the time of birth?" asked the wife.

The social worker checked the chart she was holding and said, "Two fifty-nine A.M."

After explaining why she was asking the questions, the wife asked if she could see a picture of the birth mother. When the social worker drew a photo out of the file and showed it to the couple, the wife, exclaimed, "That's the woman in my dream."

Though there is no scientific explanation for the wife's dream, the experience was real, springing from an aspect of our nature that many scientists reject or know very little about.

Our Spiritual Reality

The soul is our reality. Inherent in the soul are certain qualities that most of us admire and wish we could manifest at all times. Truthfulness, trustworthiness, love, integrity, selflessness, humility, kindness and courtesy are some of these qualities. All of them and more are latent within the soul, just as the color, fragrance, and vitality of the flower are latent within the seed. Every infant who comes into this world possesses latent virtues. This is what makes us potentially good.

The divine virtues latent within the soul are like seeds. To grow and fulfill their potential, they must be properly and regularly nourished. When they are, they become more prominent in a person's life, eventually becoming permanent fixtures, like sturdy branches to a tree; we become virtuous women and men, aware of the reality of the oneness of humankind.

Ideally, the nourishment takes the form of a home environment that stimulates the development of virtues. While teaching their children about the nature of the human being, parents must impress upon them the importance of continually nourishing their inherent virtues and must show them how it is done by their own actions. Finding the time to give youngsters undivided attention whenever interacting with them; expressing unqualified love; and as a gesture of support, holding a child's hand or placing an arm around his shoulder while talking to him are all examples of positive nourishment. When a child exhibits an attribute such as kindness or compassion, it should be enthusiastically acknowledged by an adult. A child usually values whatever makes a parent or teacher happy. Whenever issuing punishment, always focus on the act that provokes the punishment and not on the child. Before carrying out the punishment, children should understand why they are being punished so they don't repeat the unacceptable act. And when parents mistreat their children, they should always find time to apologize to them. Resorting to apology is not only an expression of respect for the child, the parent is also teaching the youngster respect by example. Of course, when we believe that the human being is purely an animal, we expect animalistic behavior; life is viewed as a jungle where might makes right and "beating out" the next guy is considered natural; loving and compassionate people are often viewed as fools, and demonstrating thoughtfulness, courtesy, and generosity are employed only as a means of achieving a selfish goal.

But a human being is more than an animal. Being a soul makes the human being potentially divine. The soul also possesses the powers of thought, comprehension, and imagination. Inner vision is another faculty of the soul. It is the source of a human being's original and intuitive ideas.

The difference between the brain and inner vision is that inner vision "knows," while the brain reasons.

Using their inner sight, many scientists see a meaningful idea unfold, and they know it is right. To prove it to their colleagues, they employ vehicles of reasoning such as scientific principles and mathematics. Helen Keller, the incomparable blind and deaf early twentieth-century poet and philosopher, had a keen inner sight; she often saw and felt something that many sighted persons never see or feel in their lifetime: "I sense a rush of ethereal rains. . . . I possess the light which shall give me vision a thousandfold when death sets me free."[5]

Clearly, the human being doesn't come into existence as a clean slate. The soul is endowed with certain powers and attributes that are to be discovered and developed. Among these powers are the yearnings to know, to love, and to be loved. To ensure good health, these yearnings must be satisfied from birth through old age. When they are neglected, we become emotionally crippled, or worse. Children are known to have died because of a lack of love. A poor student hungers for knowledge; if the yearning cannot be fulfilled in school, she will seek fulfillment elsewhere, usually on the street. Adults who stop learning and are deprived of a loving relationship usually suffer despair.

At the outset, nature assists us in satisfying these yearnings. The infant's need to know, to love, and to be loved is satisfied when he finds his mother's breast and suckles and is stroked by her. But these yearnings are to be used for an even greater purpose than simply creating healthy human relationships. The soul's impulses to know, to love, and to be loved are to be used to strengthen our connection with God. Above all, the powers of knowing and loving are to be used to know and love our Creator. Through this relationship we become greater lovers of our fellow human beings, God's children. We discover and put into practice the divinely crafted innate wisdom within us. As a consequence, we are enabled to uncover some of the mysteries that, in the past, were an enigma. Realizing that we are meant to be a source of unity, we develop a continual urge to bring people together. And we realize that we are endowed with the capacity to be a unifying force wherever we may find ourselves. It becomes evident that to be fully human we must be continually involved in developing this capacity. When that happens, we become a source of attraction to whomever we meet.

Even those who reject the reality of the soul, or who have a warped understanding of the soul, employ its powers. This is because we have no choice. Not using the powers of the soul would be like a fish's refusing to swim. The trouble is that the human being who refuses to acknowledge the true source of those powers will attribute them to some bodily function.

If the soul is focused only on the physical world, its powers will be used to carry out only physical desires. If, on the other hand, it is trained "heavenward," its powers will be used to fulfill spiritual pursuits such as developing virtues that turn women and men into the kind of humans they are meant to be—more generous than greedy, more caring than callous, more humble than vainglorious, more thoughtful than selfish. A spiritually developing person attains a penetrative sight, has the capacity to see the reality of others and hear the inner voice of the troubled human being—in other words, she hears more than words; she senses the real meanings behind the words, and is able to learn the real truth. Irrational feelings make sense when we understand what's behind them.

Though the soul is meant to be developed, humans are, as we have mentioned, endowed with free will. Those who choose to reject the notion of a soul or ignore its development can do more harm than a beast in the field because they can use thought, memory, speech, intuition, imagination—all powers of the soul—to do evil things. A gorilla is incapable of doing what Hitler or Stalin did. Thomas Aquinas, the thirteenth-century Christian theologian, once said, "One human being can do more evil than all the other species of creatures put together."[6]

Though the physical aspect of our nature is the repository and generator of our senses, it has another important function: The physical aspect demonstrates what the spiritual aspect initiates. For example, without a body to carry out our intentions, our strong desire to help an elderly person cross the street would remain nothing more than a good intention. So a healthy body is not only necessary for producing healthy children; it is essential to carrying out positive spiritual impulses.

In reality, both the physical aspect and the spiritual aspect of our nature are dependent on each other to carry out their ordained purpose, which is to create a loving and caring human being who, in turn, becomes a positive influence in the community. To live a good life is, I believe, to continually manifest the attributes of the soul in all of our interactions, regularly caring for both aspects of our nature. When this balance is maintained, each aspect is clearly defined: The spiritual aspect, which is the soul, becomes more assertive, and the physical aspect becomes more submissive. Only under such conditions are the two aspects fulfilling their ideal roles. As the soul matures, it not only initiates positive ideas but also prompts the physical aspect (our animal side) into action. The result of such a cooperative union is a highly developed conscience, which acts as a catalyst for doing good deeds, among which is an earnest effort to help others understand and internalize the principle of the oneness of humankind. This is accomplished not through coercion but through love.

Obviously, people who are unaware of their spiritual reality will not be involved in developing their soul's precious properties. Ruled by their animal-like instincts, they are unable to appreciate the reality of the oneness of humankind. To them, it is an abstraction unworthy of serious consideration. Fearful, their primary preoccupation is survival in an uncertain, highly competitive world. As a result, they tend to be extremely self-absorbed and uninterested in other people's feelings or problems, making them highly suspicious of change. This makes them susceptible to the myths that support the prevailing notion that humanity is meant to be divided into separate races and ethnic groups.

CHAPTER 4

EXPOSING THE MYTHS

The notion that blood has something to do with our ethnicity is an ancient myth that many people still accept as the truth. It is not uncommon to hear people refer to their "Irish blood," their "Jewish blood," their "Chinese blood," or their "Italian blood," and this goes on even in our age of home computers and exploration of outer space. In many circles the idea of mixing "racial bloods" is met with revulsion. There is a popular fear that racial intermarriage will weaken one's familial bloodline. Blood transfusions are avoided by many Whites for fear of receiving the blood of a Black or Asian person. For a while, the White-dominated Israeli public health system discarded every contribution of blood by dark-skinned Ethiopian Jews, fearing that it was diseased. This was done without testing the donations.

Fear of Miscegenation

Ever since the United States of America came into being, Whites, including the Founding Fathers, have exerted considerable effort to prevent the mixing of "racial bloods." State laws were passed to make racial intermarriage illegal. Abraham Lincoln announced publicly that he was opposed to marriage between Blacks and Whites.[1] The feeling among most Whites was that even so little as one drop of "Black blood" was enough to disqualify a person from being considered Caucasian.

While Whites have tried hard to uphold this belief, they have also secretly strayed from it. It was fairly common for White slave owners, including some of the Founding Fathers, to engage in sex with female slaves, many of whom bore children from such liaisons with their masters. Lots of mixing of Black and White "blood" went on for nearly two centuries in what was officially considered a racially segregated nation. This went on even though efforts were made by Colonial and state governments to block sexual encounters between the races.

In Virginia during the mid-1600s, White men who were caught engaging in sexual intercourse with Black women were flogged in public, usually before an assemblage of slaves. Such displays were intended to demonstrate to the one being flogged that he had sunk to a stature lower than that of a slave. To assure that "White blood" would not be tainted by "Black blood," public officials in the post-Civil War South established and passionately defended racial segregation without any interference from the federal government. This was achieved through a regional campaign of fear that eventually became a tradition. Organizations such as the Ku Klux Klan played a role in generating the fear by intimidating and sometimes killing those who opposed racial segregation.

When in 1954 the U.S. Supreme Court declared racial segregation in public schools unconstitutional, Yale-educated Circuit Court Judge Thomas Brady of Mississippi expressed a fear that many Whites in the North as well as the South harbored. He warned that the Supreme Court's decision would lead to "the tragedy of miscegenation." Judge Brady vowed that he would fight and die for the principles of racial purity and White womanhood rather than follow the Supreme Court's decision. He declared that God opposes racial mixing and that Whites in the South had a God-given right to keep their blood White and pure.[2]

The Myth of "Racial Bloods"

There are many Americans today who view themselves as White and have more than one drop of "Black blood" within them. Determination as to which race one belongs to is based on external factors. Not only is skin color a determining factor, but so are facial features and hair texture. Of course, there are some individuals who can pass for White but prefer to think of themselves as Black because they are aware of, and proud of, their African ancestry. Nonetheless, the great majority who can pass as White choose to do so. According to the *Ohio Journal of Science,* about 155,000 Blacks passed over the color line to become Whites during the years 1941–1950.[3] The phenomenon of "passing" continues to this day.

The need to pass as Europeans existed in America in the 1700s, especially in the Spanish-ruled areas of the Southwest, Florida, and Mexico. Without European women around them, Spanish soldiers and explorers married Indian women. Their offspring, who were called "mestizos," tried hard to obscure their Indian heritage and emphasized their "Spanish blood." The Spanish colonial government made it possible for the mestizo and even the full-blooded Indian to pass as a "superior" White person by selling "certificates of whiteness" to those who had mastered the Spanish language and culture.[4]

While the belief that blood is a key factor in determining one's ethnicity remains entrenched in most human hearts, it is a myth masquerading as the truth. In fact, it is another example of how far and how long humans can stray from the truth while believing that they are on the right course, even when authentic scientific evidence to the contrary is presented.

Actually, human blood is one of the proofs that people everywhere, regardless of skin color, hair texture, culture, and geographical location, belong to the same family or species. Only four basic blood types (A, B, AB, and O) are found in all ethnic groups. No other species' blood can be given to save the life of a human, but a White Englishman with Type O blood who needs a transfusion can receive blood from a Black Ghanaian who also has Type O blood, with successful results.

While many people still strive to keep their family bloodline "pure," feeling that racial mixing is unhealthy, scientific research does not support this belief. In fact, according to the latest research, the exact opposite is true. Hemophilia, a sex-linked blood defect that is characterized by delayed clotting, usually results from inbreeding in generation after generation. The Royal families of Europe, many of whose male offspring have suffered from the disorder, provide a case in point.[4]

Despite the prevailing attitude of suspicion toward mixing the blood of different races, it is practiced in most hospitals throughout the world. Blood banks do not classify the blood they collect as African, Asian, European, Hispanic, American Indian, French, English, Japanese, Tanzanian, or Brazilian. Nor do they classify blood according to the height of the donor. What is classified is the basic type of blood: A, B, AB, or O.

The myth that crossbreeding leads to the mongrelization of one's race ethnic group is still accepted as the truth by many people, including many educated individuals with post-graduate degrees. This belief is based on a lack of information and on fear.

Harvard biologist Richard Lewontin asserts that there is no such thing as a "pure" race:

> Anthropologists no longer try to name and define races and subraces, because they recognize that there are no "pure" human groups who have existed since the beginning of Creation as separate units. The most striking feature of global human history is the incessant and widespread migration and fusion of groups from different regions. Wholesale migration is not a recent phenomenon brought about by the development of airplanes and ships. . . . The notion that there are stable, pure races that only now are in danger of mixing under the influence of modern industrial culture is nonsense.[5]

The Reality of Crossbreeding

In reality, all human beings are "mixed," due to crossbreeding in the past, and this crossbreeding has been going on for a very long time, perhaps as long as humans have inhabited the planet. In fact, there is no such thing as a pure race. True, there have been some demented individuals such as Adolph Hitler who have tried to cultivate a "pure" race by rewriting history, inventing a new form of biology and anthropology, and promoting a campaign of forced inbreeding. Those who followed him were led to believe that they were purely Aryan. To believe the Nazi leadership, German citizens had to turn their back on history and dismiss many facts, including the fact that, in Germany between 1921 and 1925, 42 percent of all marriages involving Jews were mixed.[6] In other words, many "Aryans" were married to the very people Hitler felt were undesirable evolutionary throwbacks, worthy only of the gas chamber. And most of those "mixed" German couples had children.

In reality, the Germans, like everyone else, are a mixed people. Living in the center of Europe, their land was inevitably invaded many times over the centuries by peoples from the north, south, east, and west. Some of these invaders were Nordic types from Scandinavia; others had swarthier complexions. For example, Hannibal, the great North African general, led his army of about twenty thousand men in 216 B.C. over the Swiss Alps into what is now known as Germany. Undoubtedly, sexual forays with the native women produced some children. Ironically, after Hitler's demise there was a rash of racially mixed children born to German women, the result of the conquering Black American soldiers' marriages or romantic flings with the local ladies. Furthermore, Germany's remarkable economic recovery after World War II attracted many Turkish, Arab, Persian, and Armenian immigrants who sought steady employment. Many settled there, marrying German women and producing racially mixed children.

Even Afrikaners, the South-African "White" people of Dutch extraction who were the creators of apartheid, are not totally White—a fact that most of them would undoubtedly dispute. The fact that they are racially mixed was brought to light by Dr. N. C. Botha, an Afrikaner himself. The famous immunologist calculated that the Afrikaners have an average of 7 percent "non-white" genes. He also discovered that the three million so-called "colored" South Africans have 34 percent "White" genes.[7]

There is evidence that the Celts, the Phoenicians, the Vikings, and the Polynesians had contact with some of the indigenous peoples of the Americas long before Columbus set foot on the Caribbean island on which he first landed, believing he was just off the coast of India.[8] It is also believed that the first English-American Indian racial fusion took place on Roanoke

Island in 1585, before the arrival of the Pilgrims. When the British colony was absorbed by the local Croatoan Indians, a harmonious biracial society was established. Today's Lumbee Indians of North Carolina are believed to be the descendants of that first English-Indian merger.[9]

There were many other examples of racial mixing between Africans and Indians in North America. One of the earliest mergers took place in 1526. Five hundred Spaniards and 150 of their African slaves founded a town near the mouth of the Pee Dee River in what is today South Carolina. When the slaves revolted, killing some of their masters, the Spaniards fled to Haiti. The Blacks remained and assimilated with the native people in the region.[10] Many escaped slaves found refuge among the Seminoles in Florida, many of them finding partners and producing children.

More than five thousand Africans from Gambia, traveling at different times in different ships, crossed the Atlantic Ocean in the seventeenth century and settled as free people in what is today Honduras; many of them married local Indian people. Eighth-century African artifacts, including statues and tombs bearing carefully chiseled portraits of men with distinctly Negroid features, have been discovered in the Yucatan peninsula and in the area of Costa Rica, Honduras, and Mexico. Many words in the local languages of Central America can be traced to words that are part of West African and Nubian languages. Some Negroid characteristics have been found in the indigenous people of these areas. For example, the malaria-resistant sickle cell that is found in the blood of West Africans is often found in the blood of Central Americans. Some social scientists see this as evidence that Africans came and settled in Central America and assimilated with the local people long before Columbus's arrival in the Western Hemisphere.[11]

Nineteenth- and early twentieth-century anthropologists claimed that the Australian Aborigines were a pure race of people. It was later learned that through the centuries Papuans, Malays, Negritos, and Melanesians trickled into the Australian continent.[12] It doesn't take much for ethnic or racial mixing to take place on a grand scale. According to science writer Guy Murchie, a single indirect genetic contact between Africa and Asia in a thousand years can make every African closer than fiftieth cousin to every Chinese person.

For a long time the British aristocracy gave the impression that they were part of a pure race of specially endowed people who were superior to all others and, therefore, entitled to privileges denied everyone else. The truth is that, before the influx of Indians, Pakistanis, Malaysians, Caribbean Blacks, and Africans after World War II, all British people were an interesting composite of many different ethnicities. They were not purely White Anglo-Saxons. The indigenous people—the Beaker Folk of the Bronze Age, the Indo-European Celts, and the Picts—were creative, basically warrior-like peoples who, at times, practiced cannibalism. Over the years, Jutes, Vikings, Romans, Dutch, and Normans settled in what is today the British Isles, as did some Germanic peoples—the Saxons and Angles. Among these settlers were some of the ancestors of the present Royal family. The Spain-based Moors, who were originally from North Africa, made many trips to what is now Britain and Ireland, Ireland being their favorite spot. Romances bloomed between the exploring dark-skinned men and the Celtic lasses, producing children. That is how the "black Irish" element in the Irish population came about. There are other currents of Africa running through the body of Britain. In the 1500s there were thousands of Blacks living in England, and many of them were not slaves. These people did not simply vanish. Something very natural occurred: Black and White men and women fell in love, and babies resulted.

The Myth of Jewish Purity

Many people believe that Jews are perhaps the "purest" people alive, a feeling that is usually shared by most Jews themselves. Many even believe that there is a "Jewish look." Both ideas are false. It may be true that, to the unfamiliar eye, all Hasidic men look alike, for they all have beards and wear black hats and suits and white shirts. But under closer scrutiny, it can be seen that some are blond-haired and blue-eyed, while others are quite swarthy and have brown eyes and black hair. There are even redheads. And they come in a variety of sizes. In other parts of the world, Jews look much like the general population of the nation in which they reside. For example, in Ethiopia, the Jews have black skin and coiled hair; in Kaifeng, China, the Jews look Chinese; in Yemen, the Jews have a dark olive complexion, much like that of their Arab countrymen. Before World War II, 49 percent of the Polish Jews were light-haired,[13] and 54 percent of the Jewish children in Austria had blue eyes.[14] This proves that there is no such thing as a Jewish race.[15] Jews are a great mixture of people who share a similar religion, which, like most other religions, is splintered.

The two major divisions of Judaism are the Sephardim and Ashkenazim. Some 500,000 to 1,000,000 Sephardim are descendants of Jews who lived in Spain until they were expelled in the fifteenth century, settling in the countries—including those of North Africa—bordering the Mediterranean. A few fled to other western European countries. To escape the wrath of the Roman Catholic Inquisition, some Sephardic Jews in Spain converted to Christianity and continued secretly to practice Judaism. The Sephardim spoke a Spanish dialect that was written in Hebrew letters. Throughout the centuries they have been able to preserve their special religious traditions and rites. Today, the majority of Sephardim live in Israel.

It is believed that the Sephardim are the descendants of those Jews who were chased out of the Holy Land by the Romans about two thousand years ago. For the most part, they are a dark-haired, olive-complexioned people. When one examines their ancestral background, it is easy to understand why. The tribe of Israel was basically Semitic, which is a composite of the Cushites, who were Black; the Hittites, who were a Mongoloid type; and the Amorites, who were fair-skinned and blond. Furthermore, there is biblical evidence that the ancient Hebrews intermarried with all of these groups.[16] Abraham, who is considered the father of the Jewish people, was married to a number of women, including Hagar, an Egyptian; Joseph was married to Asnath, whose father was an Egyptian priest; Moses' wife Zipporah was a Midianite whose ancestral roots were in Arabia. Samson, the great Jewish hero, was a Philistine; King David's mother was a Moabite. As for King Solomon, whose mother was a Hittite, he sired scores of children by Edonite, Zidonian, Ammonite, Moabite, and Hittite women. One of his favorites was the daughter of an Egyptian Pharaoh. Undoubtedly, many of King Solomon's subjects followed his example and married Gentiles. During the Babylonian exile, members of Israelite priestly families married Gentile women. In short, when the Diaspora started, the Israelites were already a thoroughly hybridized people.[17]

There is considerable evidence that the approximately 15 million Ashkenazim who, before World War II, were concentrated throughout Eastern Europe are more closely related to the Hun, Uigur, and Magyar tribes than to the Semitic tribe of Israel. Most Ashkenazim, however, still believe their genetic lineage sprang from the seed of Abraham, Isaac, and Jacob.[18] It is felt that to be otherwise would somehow make them less authentic Jews and would disqualify them as members of the "Chosen People." This is not a matter that their religious leaders are willing to discuss publicly.

Nevertheless, the first Ashkenazi was the King of the Khazar kingdom, Leo IV, who converted to Judaism around 740 A.D. After his court and the military ruling class embraced the Jewish faith, Judaism became the state religion.[19]

The Khazar kingdom was a large stretch of land centered in what is known today as the Russian steppes, which extend from the Aral Sea in Asia to Ukraine in Eastern Europe. The Khazar people were a mixture of many different tribes, some Asian in origin and appearance and others Caucasian. Modern anthropologists classify the Khazars as a "Turkic" people. Actually, the term "Turkic" refers more to the language spoken by the people than to their genetic makeup. The Khazars are an amalgam of many tribes: the Huns, Alans, Avars, Bulgars, Magyars, Bashkirs, Burtas, Sabirs, Uigurs, Saragurs, Onogurs, Utigurs, Kutrigurs, Tarniaks, Kotragars, Khabars, Zabenders, Pechenegs, Ghuzz, Kumans, and Kipchaks.

The Khazars, who took their religion seriously, were fierce warriors. They were the ones who repulsed the Arab thrust northward in the mid-seventh century. The Khazar kingdom flourished until the thirteenth century, when it fell to the onslaught of Genghis Khan. The conquering Mongolian troops did what was customary in those days, and the women in the defeated land had to submit to the conqueror's sexual advances. Chances are great that Mongolian genes were added to the existing rich Khazar genetic mix.

My father, who was an Ashkenazi from Russia, had Asian facial features, high cheekbones, almond-shaped eyes, and straight black hair. His father looked Chinese or Korean. When my wife gave birth to our second son, the doctors and nurses thought he was Chinese or Korean. Undoubtedly, there was some of the Hun, who originated in western China, and some of the Mongolian in my father's gene pool.

After the Mongolian invasion, many Khazars dispersed, heading west to settle in the areas now known as Poland, Hungary, Lithuania, Latvia, Romania, and Germany. Others remained in Ukraine and Crimea. In an attempt to prevent Jews from converting Christians to Judaism, the Roman Catholic Church issued an edict forcing all Jews living in Christian lands to move to ghettoes. The rulers of those lands tried hard to enforce the papal decree. As a result, the Ashkenazim, for the most part, became ghettoized, creating a common language called Yiddish—which is a combination of medieval German, some Hebrew, Slavonic, and other elements—that is written in Hebrew characters. A Yiddish culture emerged, producing over the years a rich assortment of music and literature. The descendants of the Khazars used Yiddish as a means of linking all of the Ashkenazic ghettoes in Eastern Europe.

Unfortunately, there were some serious drawbacks to the ghettoization of the Ashkenazim. Inbreeding led to the high incidence of deficient mental capacities among the ghetto occupants.[20] Tay-Sachs disease became a congenital problem that continues to plague the Ashkenazim and their descendants today. Barred from owning land and engaging in agriculture, the ghetto Jew was forced to engage in various service trades such as tailoring and money lending. To ensure their survival, they mastered the trades they were allowed to practice. In time, they were stigmatized by many Gentiles as "cheating money lenders."

Before the ghettoization of the Ashkenazim and the Spanish persecution of the Sephardim, Jews were active and successful proselytizers of their religion, even after the birth of Christianity. Conversion was greatest during the Greco-Roman era. Prominent Italian and Greek families embraced Judaism, thus adding more Gentile genes to the Jewish gene pool. The proselytizing continued until the thirteenth century, when the Catholic Church ordered Jews to remain confined in their own communities and warned them not to interact with Christians.

Rape was another means by which diversity was added to the Jewish genetic pool. Russian Cossacks would, from time to time, sweep into Jewish villages, select the prettiest women, and leave them pregnant. The children who resulted from these escapades were brought up as Jews. But the raping—which was, in effect, a means of crossbreeding—was going on long before the Cossacks existed and long before the Mongols conquered the Khazar kingdom. The earliest Jewish settlements in Germany are believed to be the result of Roman soldiers in Palestine seizing Jewish women and bringing them back to their homeland along the Rhine River in the area of Germany. When these women produced children, many of the men fled. Faithful to their religion, the women brought up their children as Jews.

The Positive Effects of Crossbreeding

It is apparent that despite ignorance of the reality of the oneness of humankind, and despite age-old suspicions and fears of interacting with people of different ethnic groups, there has been a great deal of crossbreeding throughout the ages. It is as if a mighty force were somehow working to overcome people's fear of civil interaction with people who speak a different language, belong to a different religion, and pursue a different philosophy of life. Yet through wars, pogroms, slavery, migrations, and commercial trade, men and women of different skin colors, cultures, morays, and ethical systems have come together to produce children. Since inbreeding has such a deleterious effect on the general health of a population, crossbreeding has helped to strengthen the biological makeup of a population. Take Brazil, for example, where crossbreeding between Blacks, Whites, and Indians has been going on for nearly four hundred years. The mixed population has increased enormously, and many Brazilians of mixed ancestry have attained the highest distinction in every walk of life.

Sociologist Paolo Freire points out that "Everything leads us to believe that miscegenation was a valuable contributing factor in the formation of the Brazilian, creating the ideal type of the modern man for the tropics, the European with Negro or Indian blood mixed to revive his energy."[21] The same is true in Cuba. The healthiest and most progressive people seem to have the most varied genetic heritage.

Chances are that without crossbreeding, the human race would be less advanced intellectually, a lot weaker physically, perhaps even extinct. The point is that inbreeding is a dangerous practice. It appears to run counter to the laws of nature. Beyond the biological problems associated with inbreeding in Europe's royal families and among the ghettoized Ashkenazim, cellular and molecular biologist Theodosius Dobzhansky uncovered further evidence while studying a New Guinea tribe that was geographically and culturally isolated from other tribes. The inbreeding of the tribe resulted in the development of a deadly neuropathological condition called "kuru." Dobzhansky's study found that, of the tribe's 30,000 people, nearly 50 percent of the women contracted the genetically-inherited disease, and 10 percent of those died as a result.[22]

According to molecular biologist Shidan Lofti,

It is not a newly discovered observation that close inbreeding can produce harmful effects. . . . The more closely related human parents are, the greater the chances of inherited genetic disease. The field of medicine has long known of this concept, but the science of genetics has explained the reasons for it on a molecular level. Simply stated, it occurs as a result of the increased probability of inheritance of an allele that causes biological malfunction by offspring of closely-related parents who both have high risks of that condition. If the condition is recessive, both parents must possess the allele in order to pass it on to the offspring. If the condition is dominant, the existence of that allele by only one parent is sufficient for the offspring to inherit that condition.

Rather than randomly selecting from a wider pool of genes, deliberate close inbreeding by individuals of an "isolated" group narrows the pool of available genes for that group and produces a kind of genetic stagnation. If in such a group deleterious genes are present, the chances of offspring having harmful hereditary traits is increased.[23]

Racial Myths

There are still many Whites who believe that people of color, especially Blacks, are somehow genetically more closely related to the ape than other people are. If such people do not openly proclaim that belief, it is nevertheless a dominant factor in their overall racial outlook, often generating suspicion, fear, and hostility toward Blacks, whom they feel to be a lower form of humanity. If such people are politically correct, they are careful about whom they share this feeling with. The belief is not based on scientific studies. It is usually based on a very limited and superficial association with Blacks, the portrayal of Blacks in the mass media, and on familial folklore influenced by an assortment of age-old prejudices. Only knowledge and a sustained, meaningful association with Blacks can draw out this poisonous belief from their hearts.

Sadly, some Blacks who suffer severely from internalized racism are haunted by the thought of their being more apelike than Whites are. This is not a feeling they would want to discuss with others, or, perhaps, even admit to themselves. It is something they try to repress.

Dr. James King, a professor at New York University's medical school, debunks the idea that Blacks are genetically closer to apes. He points out that when the measurements of protein differences within the human species are compared with those between apes and humans, the latter are from twenty-five to sixty times as great as any difference between two human populations, and neither Caucasians, black Africans, nor Japanese are any nearer to the chimpanzee than either of the others. In fact, King goes on to state that Whites share more similar superficial characteristics with apes than Blacks do:

Superficial similarities between apes and men appear randomly in different human groups. So far as pigmentation is concerned, the human blacks are most apelike, but the chimpanzee is less black than some Africans. In general apes have fine, straight, and profuse hair. Among humans, these characteristics are most closely approximated in the Caucasians. Among blacks the hair is coiled and on the body it is sparse; among Mongolians it is coarse, straight and sparse. Apes have thin lips, another characteristic most closely approached among the Caucasians. In man the spine is curved inward in the small of the back; in the ape it is not. In man this characteristic is most pronounced and least apelike in African blacks. No human population is in any real sense more apelike than any other.[24]

Another myth that seems to have been accepted as fact by many people of all walks of life is that the color of a person's skin is a determining factor of one's intelligence, creativity, potential to succeed, and ability to survive. In North America and Europe, people have been led to believe that Whites are the most naturally gifted and beautiful people in the world. This belief was shared passionately and at times forcefully with Asians, Africans, Inuit, and Pacific Islanders by White colonizers from the sixteenth century to the early part of the twentieth century. The colonizers' brainwashing technique called for cutting off the colonized from their rich cultural heritage, leaving them with a sense of inferiority and a desire to be more like their rulers. All that is good in the world, they were led to believe, was the result of White invention. Sadly, Christian missionaries played a major role in such brainwashing.

In reality, peoples living in all parts of the world have contributed to the development of humankind. The idea that Whites alone are the master contributor to this development is a myth that most Whites still adhere to, unfortunately. This belief is a classic example of prejudice as emotional commitment to ignorance.

American Indian Contributions

The American Indians, whom the European settlers considered savages, were highly advanced in a number of areas. Their skills benefited the white colonizers in many ways. For example, aside from the Thanksgiving Day story about the Indians' keeping the Pilgrims from starving to death by supplying them with turkeys, pumpkins, potatoes, squash, and corn, we know that three-fifths of all of the foods the world enjoys today were being produced by Indian agriculturists. Among those important foods were the tomato, the potato, corn, chilies, and chocolate.

The Indians had also produced medical remedies that helped to cure diseases plaguing the Europeans. When sixteenth-century French navigator and explorer Jacques Cartier noticed that Indians who contracted scurvy survived while many of his own men were dying from the disease, he approached the Huron medicine men for their remedy. It was a concoction made of extracts from evergreen trees that contained a massive dose of vitamin C. But the Hurons did not receive credit for discovering the cure for scurvy. Instead, a Scottish naval officer, James Lind, got the credit. He read about Cartier's experience, did some research of his own, and realized it was the vitamin C in the Hurons' concoction that cured the scurvy. He shared what he had learned with the British Admiralty, which ordered every naval vessel to have every sailor take a daily dose of lime juice. As for Cartier, he showed his appreciation to the Hurons by kidnapping their chief, Donnaconna, and a number of other Indians, hoping that they would lead him to sources of gold in their territory.[25]

The Incas knew how to prevent goiter as effectively as the Hurons knew how to prevent scurvy. They harvested kelp, which has a high iodine content, from the Pacific Ocean. After drying the seaweed, they transported it throughout the Andes, encouraging people to use it as a food supplement. Unlike the Europeans, the Incas did not suffer from goiter problems.[26]

The Indians of Oregon and northern California used the bark of the Rhamnus purshiana shrub to produce a laxative that is still used today in modern medicine. Seventeenth-century Spanish soldiers suffering from constipation viewed the laxative as a miracle drug. In his book *Indian Givers,* anthropologist Jack Weatherford points out that

The Indians of North America used the bark of the poplar or willow tree to make a liquid capable of curing headaches and other minor pains. Only centuries later with the discovery of aspirin as a coal-tar derivative was it found that the active ingredient salicin resembled what we now know as aspirin or acetylsalicylic acid. Such a simple medication remains as a good example of many American Indian gifts that western medical science failed to recognize and then had to invent independently through a laborious and expensive process of research.[27]

While the Indians of the Americas created scores of other medicines, they also practiced many other medical arts that were unknown to Europeans at the time. Andean Indians were performing a sophisticated form of brain surgery.[28] The Aztecs had organized a sophisticated system of medical specialists for the diagnosis of disease, its treatment, and the manufacture of drugs. Surgery was also included in the system.[29]

Indians made significant achievements in other fields besides medicine. The Mayans excelled in astronomy, architecture, and mathematics. A group of North American Indians created the first democracy in the Western Hemisphere. George Washington's great-great-grandparents had not yet been born when the League of Iroquois, which united five previously warring nations, was formed. About two centuries later, a sixth nation was added to the league, which lived in peace for centuries. This democracy came about through a vision experienced by an enlightened Huron, Deganwidah, and was carried out by his energetic spokesman, Hiawatha. They crafted a constitution, The Great Law of Peace, which became the unifying force that preserved the peace. Aware of a good thing, America's Founding Fathers plagiarized the Iroquois constitution when it came time to create one of their own (however, James Madison and his colleagues refused to include in the U.S. Constitution the Iroquois belief in the equality of men and women, and American women did not win the right to vote until 1920).[30] The American Indians had their share of seers, military leaders, philosophers, prophets, and enlightened rulers, including Sitting Bull, Crazy Horse, Chief Seattle, Black Elk, Buffalo Calf Woman, Deganwidah, Quetzalcoatl, and Chief Joseph of the Nez Percé, to name only a few.

African Contributions

The Africans have also made significant contributions to the development of humankind. Despite the Europeans' view of Africa as the "dark" continent, parts of Africa were quite enlightened when Europe was ensnared in its Dark Ages. Between the sixth and thirteenth centuries, West Africa, consisting of the kingdoms of Ashanti, Ghana, Mali, Benin, and Songhay, was flourishing. More than 100 million people lived in the area. Their farmers were using metal implements at a time when most of their European counterparts were still using sticks. Iron was discovered in Africa.[31] In East Africa, the Tanzanians were producing carbon steel before the birth of Christ. Black metallurgists produced steel surgical instruments fine enough that Black surgeons could perform eye operations long before the European Renaissance. Imhotep, a black Egyptian physician, practiced medicine two thousand years before the birth of Hippocrates, whom Europeans refer to as the "father of medicine."[32] Most of the gold in Europe was purchased from Africans who mined and processed the precious metal. Besides being leading exporters of gold, West Africans had developed commercial routes reaching into the Middle East, where merchants favored African textiles. In Timbuktu, a center of enlightenment, southern European scholars came to learn from Black philosophers. A sophisticated system of jurisprudence was practiced in that city, and young men throughout the Muslim world went there to study law and surgery at the University of Sankore, whose medical institute performed successful cataract removal operations and developed an anesthetic that would keep patients unconscious during surgery. A vaccination against smallpox was introduced into North America in 1721 by a slave who brought the method over from Africa.

"In Timbuktu," Leo Africanus, a Christianized Moor who visited the city in the sixteenth century, said,

> there are numerous judges, doctors and clerics, all receiving good salaries from the king. He pays great respect to men of learning. There is a big demand for books in manuscript, imported from Barbary. More profit is made from the book trade than from any other business.[33]

West Africa was not a vast jungle with people living in trees. It had large urban centers where remarkable achievements were made in ceramics, weaving, and sculpture. After visiting a leading port city in Benin in around 1602, a Dutch merchant wrote,

> The Towne seemeth to be very great, when you enter it. You go into a great broad street, not paved, which seemeth to be seven or eight times broader than the Warmoes Street in Amsterdam. . . . The houses in this Towne stand in good order, one close and even with the other, as the houses in Holland stand.[34]

Early Africans also built ships that could carry as much as eighty tons, one of which is known to have transported a cargo of elephants from Kenya to China in the thirteenth century.

It was the Moors, black and brown people from North Africa, conquerors of Spain, who established the first European university, the University of Cordoba. It was not only a great seat of learning, but a center of toleration as well. The Jews of Spain, who had been persecuted by the Christians, were not only allowed to study there, but became some of its greatest professors. In fact, the great Maimonides taught there.

Much of the wisdom shared with the world by the classical Greeks originated in Egypt, an African country.

While the people of Africa have contributed to the development of humankind, they, like all other peoples, were not perfect. Like the Europeans, Asians, and American Indians, they had their faults. They maintained armies and fought wars. Slavery existed in Africa, even in the enlightened kingdoms of West Africa. However, their form of slavery was not as dehumanizing as the form maintained in the Americas by European settlers. Slaves in Africa were more like the serfs of Europe. An African slave could marry, could own property, could serve as a witness at a trial, could take an oath that was fully respected by the authorities, and could even become an heir to his master. In the Ashanti kingdom, in fact, most slaves were adopted into the master's family.[35]

African-American Contributions

Despite slavery, Jim Crowism, and continuing racial discrimination, Americans of African descent have been able to enrich the land of their birth in remarkable ways. Most people are aware of their musical contributions through the likes of Marian Anderson, Paul Robeson, Duke Ellington, John Burkes (Dizzy) Gillespie, and many other gifted musicians who created original musical forms such as jazz and rhythm and blues. African Americans' contributions in the fields of dance and drama are also well known, as are their share of renowned peacemakers and human-rights advocates such as Sojourner Truth, Frederick Douglass, Harriet Tubman, W. E. B. DuBois, Malcolm X, and the Nobel Prize laureates Dr. Martin Luther King, Jr., and

Ralph Bunche. In literature, novelists James Baldwin, Richard Wright, Alice Walker, and Toni Morrison (a Nobel Prize winner), and poets Robert Hayden, Langston Hughes, and Maya Angelou have won international acclaim. But little is known of African-American scientific contributions.

The mathematician and surveyor Benjamin Bannecker built the first clock in the United States and laid out the city of Washington, D.C. Norbert Rillieux revolutionized the sugar refining industry; Lewis Temple invented the toggle harpoon; Jan Matzeligen invented the machine for mass production of shoes; Elijah McCoy developed self-lubricating systems for locomotives and steam engines, as well as for air brakes. Among Granville T. Woods's many inventions were railways telegraphy, the overhead conductory system for electrical railways, and the third rail used by subway systems; Lewis Latimer developed a process for making electric lamp elements that made his lamp run much longer than those of Thomas Edison. Latimer also supervised the installation of electric light systems in new York City, Philadelphia, Montreal, and London. Garrett A. Morgan invented the gas mask and the traffic light; Frederick McKinley Jones adapted silent projection to the "talkies"; Dr. George Washington Carver developed some 325 products from peanuts, 118 products from the sweet potato, 75 products from pecans, hundreds from cornstalks, from clays, and from cotton; Dr. Ernest E. Just was the first to discover that the cell's nucleus is not the only determinant of heredity; Dr. Percy L. Julian developed a synthetic cortisone and other important therapeutic drugs for the treatment of arthritis, glaucoma, miscarriages, male hormonal disorders, and cancer; Dr. Floyd A. Hall developed new ways to sterilize foods, spices, and medical supplies; Dr. Daniel Hale Williams performed the first open-heart surgery; Dr. William Hinton was an international authority on venereal diseases; Dr. Louis T. Wright was the first to experiment with the antibiotic Aureomycin on humans; and millions of people are alive today because of Dr. Charles R. Drew's discovery of blood plasma for transfusions.

Persistent Myths

Despite the achievements of American Indians and Blacks, there still persists among many Whites the belief that Africans and Native Americans are inherently less intelligent than they themselves are, that this is somehow a genetic reality. Some White scholars share this belief. Unfortunately, this position received a tremendous boost when *The Bell Curve: Race, Intelligence and the Future of America,* by Richard J. Herrnstein and Charles Murray, was published. The authors argue that Africans are congenitally inferior to Caucasians, basing their argument primarily on the results of IQ tests and other standardized tests. Herrnstein and Murray try to establish the existence of a cognitive elite.

Popular conclusions of this sort present a problem. Using the IQ test to measure native intelligence is too narrow a gauge, for it fails to take into account the emotional condition of those taking the test. It also fails to account for one's educational and cultural background, as well as one's home environment—all very important considerations. Psychologist George Pransky points out that a person's mood affects his or her thinking ability. When in a low mood, a person's thinking is narrowly focused, usually directed at himself, making him extremely self-absorbed and thus unable to see the big picture of life. In this condition, one is unable to think clearly when facing problems of the moment; his judgment is usually faulty, and he is more apt to make mistakes, sometimes costly mistakes. Anger, Pransky adds, has a similar effect on a person, as does low self-esteem.[36] It can be inferred that when a person taking an IQ test is a victim of internalized racism, he is likely to be full of doubts about his abilities, suffering from a sense of inferiority, and may deeply resent being Black or an American Indian. Such a person is not going to be in the proper frame of mind to perform well on a standardized test. Pransky's point is that the lower the mood, the lower the intelligence; the higher the mood, the higher the intelligence. In other words, intelligence is a fluctuating force.

A classical example of the same principle can be seen in the results of mental tests given to American soldiers by psychologists during World War I. The psychologists were surprised to find that Jewish troops who had immigrated to the United States from Eastern Europe scored much lower than their Gentile counterparts did. They were surprised because they were aware of the Jews' reputation for intellectual superiority. Within a decade, however, American Jews were scoring above the national average on mental tests, and at present they tend to score far above the national average.[37]

Why did the immigrant Jewish soldiers score low on the mental tests? It had nothing to do with their genetic makeup or with their genetic stock. Having come from a predominately immigrant urban Jewish neighborhood in the United States, a neighborhood in which standard English was not spoken, the soldiers probably felt uncomfortable taking the mental test. The fact that those who were monitoring the test were of the dominant culture—"real Americans"—must have heightened the immigrant soldiers' anxiety. They found themselves in a strange place, with strange people, doing something that might result in their facing difficult problems, perhaps even deportation. For the Jewish soldiers who were more familiar with Yiddish than English, the testing place was not conducive to a high mood.

Today many Blacks, Hispanics, and American Indians taking standardized mental tests face the same uneasiness and anxiety that plagued the World War I Jewish soldiers. Their internalized racism sets off feelings of self-doubt, insecurity, and pending failure.

Unfortunately, so much has been written and said about Blacks' performing poorly on standardized intelligence tests that many of them enter the testing room expecting to do poorly. And whatever they fear will happen usually happens. Doing poorly on these tests has become a tradition in most Black communities, especially in poor urban neighborhoods.

But there is another concern that needs to be addressed, and that is the nature of the standardized tests themselves. Are they a true measure of intelligence? The classical IQ test only measures a person's analytical ability. In other words, it reveals a person's ability to think critically, but it fails to reveal a person's creative, intuitive, and practical skills and capacities. Unfortunately, we have been conditioned to believe that those who think well analytically are the smartest people. Education has, therefore, placed greater value on tearing down ideas than on generating constructive ideas. Considering Thomas Edison's limited educational background, it is doubtful that he would have performed well on a current standardized intelligence test, but few would debate his intelligence.

The ability to disprove a theory is held in high esteem in university circles. There is nothing wrong with possessing sharp analytical skills; they serve an important purpose. What is wrong is a lack of balance. Young people preparing for college emphasize the development of their analytical capacities and skills over everything else. Their schools usually reinforce this emphasis on analytical thinking—after all, a school's academic reputation hinges on how well its students do on national standardized tests. Because high test scores are one of the requirements for admission to the most prestigious colleges and universities, economically secure families often spend thousands of dollars to ensure that their children perform well on the tests. This is a privilege that most Black, Hispanic, and American-Indian students cannot afford.

More and more leading psychologists are acknowledging that the conventional methods of measuring intelligence are extremely limited. Yale University psychologist Robert Sternberg has observed that those who enter his graduate program with the highest IQs and entrance exam scores often do not do the best work in the long run. In fact, many of them end up ranking in the lower half of their class, for they lack the ability to generate their own theories and experiments. Tearing down other people's ideas and strong memorization skills are not necessary to creative thinking. At the same time, those students who possess exceptional creative abilities have done well in Sternberg's program. The fact that they entered the program with modest test scores did not deter them in any way from excelling.[38]

Harvard's Howard Gardner views intelligence through a sharper lens than the traditionalists do, and more and more prominent psychologists are coming to appreciate what Gardner sees. He believes that there are multiple intelligences, comprising seven abilities, which are distinct and relatively independent:

a) linguistic intelligence, used in reading a novel, writing a poem or an article, or generating an extemporaneous talk; b) logical-mathematical intelligence, used in solving mathematical problems, proving logical theorems, or completing categorical or other forms of syllogisms; c) spatial intelligence, used in finding one's way in unfamiliar terrain, figuring out how to fit suitcases into a trunk of a car, or figuring out where is a playing field a baseball batter's fly ball will land; d) musical intelligence, used in remembering a tune, singing a song, or composing a sonata; e) Bodily-kinesthetic intelligence, used in dancing ballet, performing gymnastics, or playing tennis; f) interpersonal intelligence, used in figuring out what other people mean from what they say, decoding what their facial expressions communicate, or deciding what is appropriate to say in an interaction with a superior; and g) intrapersonal intelligence, used in understanding why one takes rejection so poorly, why one tends to be overconfident in certain instances, or why one has failed in achieving an important personal goal.[39]

Gardner offers evidence from diverse sources to support his theory, including studies of brain damage, psychometric and experimental studies, and studies of psychological development.

The Effects of Internalized Racism

Meanwhile, people of color continue to be victimized by traditional intelligence tests. Their test results continue to reinforce the widespread internalized racism among America's minorities, and this internalized racism among Black, Hispanic, and American-Indian children is a real problem. It is an entrenched barrier to human development that thwarts intellectual growth.

In the early 1950s, Drs. Mamie and Kenneth Clark, psychologists, highlighted the problem of internalized racism in a telling psychological study. They tested three-to seven-year-old Black children in several American cities to determine how extensive the wound of internalized racism is. They ushered them into a room with a display of Black and White dolls. The children were told, "Give me the doll you like best; give me the nice doll; give me the doll that looks bad; and give me the doll that is the nice color." The great majority of the children preferred the White dolls.

Nearly forty years later, after the African-American community had been exposed to many "Black is beautiful" campaigns, the test was repeated—with no significant change in the results. Constant exposure to positive advertising campaigns cannot erase what is continuously reinforced unwittingly at home, in school, and in society in general.[40]

Stanford University social psychologist Claude M. Steele discovered through various studies that Black children usually enter school with two fears: the fear of being devalued and the fear of exposing their lack of ability. These children enter school in a low mood, emotionally insecure, prime candidates for failure.[41]

Harvard psychiatrist John Woodall, a veteran observer of the impact of racism on America's minorities, states that many Blacks lack the will to try to improve their lot, because they have been conditioned to be more sure of their dependence and incompetence then of their inherent strengths. The conditioning has been so thorough that even among those few Blacks who "make it" in the White person's world, there are some who are still haunted by doubts of their ability to succeed. They wonder if they would have been able to make it without the assistance of affirmative action. Dr. Woodall points out that

The disabling of the natural cycle of personality development is the dynamic that racism plays upon. And this outcome is one of the chief legacies of the disease of racism.

A society that conveys to children of color in unnumbered ways that they are inherently inferior stacks the deck against the child as it would any child. The years of overt and subtle messages conveying the inferiority of Blacks weighs heavily in the balance. By adolescence, it is not necessarily clear at all to a Black child that they possess inherent strengths that are of value to a larger society. As they would for anyone, these messages hinder the mature expansion of the child's identity. There are at least two consequences that act as intractable symptoms of racism. The first affects the individual identity in that the person becomes trapped in their sense of personal inadequacy by the paralysis of their motivation. The second, is that it becomes infinitely harder for the individual to identify beyond the identity group of their race. The result of these two is an ingrained sense of despair reflected in the fact that twice as many Blacks as Whites commit suicide, and the epidemic of violence in the Black community.[42]

While Dr. Martin Luther King, Jr., was not a psychologist, he was a keen social observer with a highly cultivated intuition that helped him see what others, including governmental and educational leaders, were unable to see: "Because the society, with unmitigated cruelty, has made the Negro's color anathema, every Negro child suffers a traumatic emotional burden when he encounters the reality of his black skin."[43]

When a minority child is traumatized in his classroom, his teacher is unaware of what is happening within the youngster's brain. This is because the teacher responds only to the child's outer expression. The child is not aware either: he feels uncomfortable and does not know why. He feels out of place and wants to be elsewhere. At times he wants to flee his classroom, for it is too painful to stay. In such a state of mind it is difficult to learn.

While trying to find out why so many Polynesian youth were dropping out of Hawaiian high schools, human developmentalist Kenneth Yamamoto gained some insights as to what was happening to traumatized minority school children. Neuroscientist Dr. Paul Herron of the University of Tennessee Medical School corroborates Yamamoto's thesis, as does Harvard's John Woodall.

Yamamoto points out that when a minority student plagued by self-doubt and feelings of inferiority steps into a classroom, it becomes a factory of failure. The student is often seized by an urge to flee. This is nature's way of telling the student to escape from a situation that is intellectually and emotionally destructive. When the student does not heed the urge and remains in class, he will, in time, find himself unable to think and reason clearly. Eventually, he won't be able to reason at all. This scary condition is the result of the shutting down of the brain's cerebral cortex, which is the seat of thought. When that happens, the part of the brain that controls our emotions takes over and sets off a fight-or-flight reaction. Those who want to flee either fall asleep in class or are so disengaged emotionally that the teacher feels compelled to send them to the principal for punishment. Those who want to fight become extremely angry and prone to violence. They know something bad has happened to them, but they are unable to explain the terrible feeling. They are usually seized by an urge to strike out at an enemy, and their inner voice cries out, "I hate this class, I hate this teacher, I hate this school." The teacher who does not hear the desperate soul's inner cry responds to the outward expression of the seething student and, out of self-defense, labels him a behavioral problem, placing him in a special track for emotionally disturbed uneducatables. While there, the troubled student may be given a mind-numbing drug that is designed to keep him from harming himself and others. Tragically, students like him are branded "dummies," a brand they usually carry through the rest of their lives.

What has just been described is no exaggeration. It is commonplace. Our cities and towns are packed with adults of all ages who have been psychologically abused in schools, never realizing their intellectual potential, never developing their native intelligence. Many of these victims bow to the educators' evaluations, accepting the idea that they are stupid. They are left bereft of hope. As a consequence, most spend the rest of their lives looking for ways to dull the pain, trying to bury the ugly memories of their experiences. Those who refuse to accept the educators' evaluations usually resist until they get into trouble with the law. Thus it should come as no surprise that one-third of all African-American males between the ages of twenty and twenty-nine are either in jail, on parole, or on probation. Of course, there are those young Black, Indian, or Hispanic men who possess a special resiliency that has allowed them to transcend the effects of being brought up in a ghetto plagued by poverty and heavy drug usage, and they are pursuing successful professions and maintaining healthy families. But they are a distinct minority.

What I have just described is not meant to be an indictment of all American educators. Most are people of goodwill. The trouble is that they have been trained to assess intelligence through IQ tests, rarely taking into account the students' emotional condition and cultural background when taking the tests. A youngster's mood—not his skin color—is an important factor in determining his intelligence at the time of testing.

Hope for Change

The challenge that teachers face is how to lift the child's mood from low to high. Studies have been done that show how this can be achieved. Neuroscientists at the University of California at Irvine discovered in 1993 through a series of experiments that music is a safe mood enhancer; it actually helps build and strengthen connections among nerve cells in the cerebral cortex, thus sharpening the test-taker's thinking ability. By exposing students to Mozart before taking IQ tests, their scores were boosted by roughly nine points.[44]

Modern science has discovered that, beginning in infancy, if children experience a lack of affection and educational stimulation they will usually perform poorly in school and will have a proclivity toward violence. In a paper presented in Chicago on June 13, 1996, at the "Brain Development in Young Children: New Frontiers for Research, Policy and Practice" conference, science writer Ronald Kotulak points out,

> The amazing discovery of the brain's plasticity—its ability to physically rewire itself to become smarter—makes mental stimulation, in the long run, more essential to the body than food. That the brain thrives with good nourishment is a concept that has profound significance for individual achievement and for the way parents raise their children.
>
> The brain's food is education. Just as the food we eat gives our immune systems the strength to fight off life-threatening infectious germs, education protects us against bad choices. In effect, education acts like a vaccine that boosts our mental powers, making us more resistant to illness and premature aging. . . .
>
> Just as some people fail to get vaccinated against common childhood infections, others fail to take advantage of the immunizing effects of education. Half of all high school students in Chicago and some other large cities, for instance, fail to graduate.
>
> The toll this takes on the brain is staggering. Children born to mothers who have less than 12 years of education have a fourfold increased risk of mental retardation, said Dr. Marshalyn Yeargin-Allsop, a medical epidemiologist at the Center for Disease Control's Division of Birth Defects and Developmental Disabilities.
>
> "This regardless of race," she said, "White children had the same fourfold risk as black children if their mothers didn't complete high school.

"A CDC study of more than 1,000 children showed that mild re-
tardation, defined as having an IQ between 50 and 70, occurs at the
rate of nearly one in 100 children. The biggest factor for mild retarda-
tion is the mother's low educational level, which far exceeds the risk
posed by poverty.

"About 22 percent of all births in this country (America) are to
mothers with less than a high school education," Yeargin-Allsop said.
"These women often do not know how to provide stimulation—such
as talk, toys, and physical activity—to their infants, which can lead
to stunting of the brain during the crucial first three years of life," she
explained.[45]

The myth that one racial group is naturally superior to another in intelligence is not only unfounded, it has fueled and aided the spread of racism.
It has reinforced the unsubstantiated but thoroughly accepted feeling of
superiority and inferiority among the oppressors and the oppressed. The
most reputable scientists agree that this myth is absolutely groundless. Behavioral geneticist Dr. Jerry Hirsch has declared, "the attempt to measure
'racial' differences in intelligence is impossible and therefore worthless."[46]

Why is it "impossible" and "worthless"? Because all humans are mixed.
There is a little of Africa, Asia, Europe, and the Americas in all of us. True,
most of us have more of one than the others; nevertheless, we have some of
all. We cannot deny that there are cultural differences and that these differences can be a factor in the development of intelligence, but we know
through scientific research that children from different cultural backgrounds
growing up in a similar range of environments show no significant differences in intelligence.[47]

CHAPTER 5

GENDER EQUALITY

True unity of the human family cannot be attained until true equality is practiced. This principle applies not only to race relations, but also to gender relations.

Gender Myths

The treatment of women has, for centuries, been driven by the myth that women are the weaker and, therefore, inferior sex. This myth contributed mightily to the creation of age-old norms regarding gender that continue to prevail in most of the world today. These norms are largely responsible for today's fractured view of gender roles. For centuries, the term "the weaker sex" has been synonymous with inherent inferiority. This attitude has become so deeply ingrained in peoples' consciousness that they have lower expectations for girls than for boys. They believe that women are incapable of achieving what Albert Einstein or George Washington Carver achieved. Female duties have therefore come to be considered less essential and less important than those of their male partners. Women have long been considered too simpleminded and emotional to engage in community policy development or to participate in planning defensive strategies. To this day, women have been conditioned to believe that they are inherently less suited to mathematics and science than men are; that they cannot handle pressure or stress as well as men do; that they lack the organizational abilities that men possess; that they are scatterbrained and too emotional to hold highly responsible positions; that men are naturally better administrators, athletes, and chess players.

Such beliefs have been passed on and reinforced from generation to generation. As a consequence, our views of women have been shaped by a series of myths that have long been accepted as fundamental truths. As with the myths associated with racial prejudice, people have become emotionally attached to these myths about gender.

Discrediting the Myths

There were some cases in the distant past in which traditional gender roles were reversed, thus discrediting the myth that women were the weaker sex. In ancient Sparta, women were the dominant sex; only they could own property. This was also true among the Iroquois as well as the Kamchadales of Siberia. According to historian C. Meiners, "When women ruled in Kamchatka, the men not only did the cooking but all of the housework, docilely doing everything assigned to them."[1] An ancient Egyptian man would have been proud of himself if he could do a woman's work—that is, to be a tall, swashbuckling soldier. The Greek historian Herodotus revealed who was the dominant sex in ancient Egypt:

With them the women go to market, the men stay home and weave.

The women discharged all kinds of public affairs. The men dealt with domestic affairs. Men were not allowed to undertake war service or any of the functions of government. Nor were they allowed to fill any public office which might have given them more spirit to set themselves against women. The children were handed over immediately after birth to the men, who reared them on milk.

In Abyssinia and in Lapland, men did what seems to us today to be women's work. The Roman historian Tacitus points out that the early Teutons living in what is now Germany did all of the work usually ascribed to modern men, hunting and farming while their husbands cared for the house. The family heirlooms, a harnessed horse, a powerful spear, a sword, and shield were passed on to the women, who were the fighters.

That those civilizations which were managed by women proved to be more graceful and kind than those controlled by men is worthy of note. This was true among the Mycenaean Greeks and Etruscans. Women proved their ability to govern as far back as three thousand years ago. For forty-two years, Semiramis of Assyria ruled what is believed to be the first stable civilization in Asia Minor. This female ruler, who was noted for her bravery, especially on the battlefield, believed that the only way to have a better world is to have more compassionate and caring people—a belief Albert Einstein shared with his contemporaries in the twentieth century.[2]

There is no modern-day Semiramis. While women today are making some headway toward equal status with men in some areas of the world, most women still function as second-class citizens, unfulfilled human beings. There are still cultures that simply expect girls and women to endure sexual slavery, being beaten and burned, traded as beasts of burden, or treated as household slaves or mere spoils of war.

How the Myths Originated

Male dominance came into being as the result of a combination of ancient secular and religious beliefs and practices that helped to establish certain behavioral patterns and ways of life. Perhaps the greatest influence stems from the patriarchal belief systems of the ancient Hebrews and Romans, which called for women to be subservient to men because of their "inherent inferiority" to them. Early Christian and Islamic leaders vigorously reinforced this attitude.

Because people have been taught for centuries that it is God's will for men to dominate women, that belief has become sacrosanct. Any interest in defying what is believed to be God's will is quickly suppressed; thus, changing attitudes is not easy, even when evidence is provided that God never called for males to dominate females. It is like trying to remove from a White person's heart the feeling of superiority toward Blacks.

When men make a concerted effort to help women advance, they are likely to find themselves becoming more compassionate and empathetic. Such changes usually lead to the development of a greater self-awareness, which enables them to experience a freedom they never knew they had been deprived of.

The High Price of Inequality

As toddlers, boys are conditioned to suppress their feelings. Their mothers, as a rule, disconnect from them emotionally far earlier than they do from their daughters in an effort to prevent them from becoming "sissies." In the past, such behavior on the part of mothers has served the useful purpose of conditioning their sons to function well on the battlefield.

In most societies today, boys still undergo some sort of "masculinization" initiation. The South African Black political leader Nelson Mandela has described how, as a boy in South Africa, he hid his agony as a ceremonial spear ripped through his foreskin. In that painful moment, he had to cry out a word that meant "I am a man." In New Guinea, a similar ritual requires boys to push reeds up their noses until they bleed. On American playgrounds, boys are routinely exposed to the torments of bullies and are frequently forced to hurt weaker boys to protect their own status.

Through the centuries, boys have been conditioned to be aggressive. An impulse to hurt and, if need be, to kill, was instilled in them. Before the twentieth century, the development of this instinct served a practical purpose. Young men became hunters who killed animals for food and their skins, which were used to make clothing. But the wish to kill turned into a "sport." Noted psychiatrist Dr. Karl Menninger, who calls aggression a morbid, psychic aberration, delves into the mind of the modern-day hunter who hunts for fun:

Reflect on the psychology of the hearty, friendly, exuberant fellow who can write with such pride the following account, referring to the gouging and tissue avulsions causing pain of the sort that, in a human being, would evoke screams or choking moans. But, says this gleeful fellow: ". . . My heart started to pound. This was the buck I was setting for. I raised my old rifle, and when the deer was broadside, I let go my first shot. It proved good. He dropped to his knees, but was up in an instant and on his way. As I hurriedly pumped in another cartridge, the buck jumped into the stream and was bounding through icy shallows to my side. I let my second shot go, and heard the solid thump of the 255 gram bullet as it hit home. But he kept right on coming. I heard my third shot smack against his ribs, but no use. . . . I let him have another slug when he was broadside. It slowed him somewhat but it didn't stop him. I let my fifth and last shot go. He reared back on his hind legs and turned around trotting in my direction. About ten paces away, the legs slipped from under him and he rolled against a rotten log and lay still. He had enough holes in him, as all of my five slugs hit home, but I don't believe my last four would have been necessary. My first shot had done the work. It hit low on front quarters, passed through and shattering the heart. That accounted for the crazed action."[3]

Dr. Menninger points out that American hunters not only hunted animals:

Some will hold, as did the early American colonists, that animals (like Indians) have no souls and are here for the pleasure and benefit of men. For over 200 years it was considered perfectly all right to have a little fun in the dull days of winter hunting down Indians and their wives and children and shooting them on the run or on their knees. For documentation of this favorite sport of the whites in Northern Canada, take a look at the article in *Macleans*'s for October 10, 1959. The unarmed quarry was routed out of tents in the dead of winter before they got dressed, and driven naked out on the frozen lakes, where they were easier to see. Men, women and little children were shot down like jack rabbits or coyotes. This popular amusement went on for two centuries, and no white man was ever prosecuted for it. But a whole nation of handsome, proud and beautiful Indians (the Beothucks) was extinguished.[4]

The hunting impulse that has been ingrained in most American males is still very much alive. It isn't girls who receive toy guns, and at times real guns, for Christmas. There are more guns in the country's homes than there are families. In fact, there are more than 250 million guns in circulation in the United States and most of them are owned by men. The urge to hurt and kill is not part of the woman's makeup—they have been conditioned to be nurtures. None of the mass killings that have taken place in American schools in the past two years were executed by girls. It was boys, with a passion for guns and with easy access to them, who did the killing, often targeting girls. For example, in Jonesboro, Arkansas, the two boys, ages eleven and thirteen, killed four students and one teacher, all females. The boys zeroed in on the girls coming out of class after the two boys had set off a fire alarm. One of the girls had recently broken up with the older boy. Before shooting her, he cried out, "No girl breaks up with me!"

The combination of an ingrained impulse to hurt and repressed feelings which generates anger, frustration, and inner pain in boys, turns many of them into walking time-bombs. Instead of releasing their pent-up true feelings, they resort to deviant behavior, and at a time of desperation, will turn to the gun.

Men have paid a price to measure up to society's idea of manhood. According to psychotherapist Terrance Real, many boys grow up suffering from depression that shows up not only in the classic symptoms of withdrawal and lethargy, but also in overbearing and violent behavior that usually goes undiagnosed.[5]

When freed from the cage of "masculinization," men are able to express a fuller range of the feelings with which all humans are endowed. As a consequence, they begin to function as more complete human beings. They are able to freely express latent spiritual qualities such as compassion, tenderness, and responsiveness, and they are able to shed tears when the urge to cry sweeps over them. They are no longer captives of convention. Aspects of their true nature that have been stifled since early childhood are discovered and used in negotiating the challenges of everyday life. Furthermore, their communities benefit from their new lease on life. Instead of taking the traditional "macho" position on social issues, these men resort to a more humane approach, leading in the end to less conflict and more unity of thought in the community.

By playing the traditional female role, women have paid an even greater price than men. Forced by custom to believe that they are inherently inferior to men, most women are left unfulfilled as human beings. Not only are they treated by males as if they were only a notch or two above a beast of burden, but their creative and intellectual potential is either ignored or barely developed. Finding themselves in this state, many women learn to suppress their desire to break out of the traditional mold. They have no faith that their situation can change, because men like the way things are. Rebellion would prove too painful. Left in a state of helplessness and hopelessness, they plunge into a state of depression that is often concealed from the males in their lives, lest they become upset with them. And that could lead to a situation worse than their present one. This kind of coping usually leads to anger that is turned inward, robbing women of self-esteem.

For centuries, women have been relegated to the kitchen and the nursery, where they have been expected to make life as comfortable and pleasurable as possible for their husbands. In many ways, a woman's life could be compared to that of a lioness that spends her time finding and preparing food and caring for her children while papa spends his time protecting the living space, sleeping, flexing his muscles, and procreating the species.

Even in materially and socially advanced countries such as the United States, women continue to struggle to achieve equal status with men. While there have been many advancements, overcoming the age-old myths and beliefs has not been easy, and much remains to be accomplished. There is still a rush of fear that races through an airline passenger when he or she learns the pilot is a woman. In many respects, overcoming gender prejudice is like trying to overcome racial prejudice. These beliefs have evolved into irrational, fixed ideas and feelings.

A Brief American Historical Perspective

A certain social pattern was set from the first day Europeans set foot on the North American continent. In Colonial and early nineteenth-century America, as elsewhere in the world, women were regarded as inferior beings and treated as chattels. They, as well as their children, property, and earnings belonged by law solely to their husbands. Various legal and social barriers made divorce almost unthinkable. Legally, American women were, in most respects, on a par with criminals, the insane, and slaves. During the Colonial period, women had no political rights and were relegated to an inferior social position. When the Declaration of Independence and the Constitution were written, they made no mention of women. It was understood by all where women ranked in the social stratum. In 1818, Thomas Jefferson, who was perhaps the most enlightened Founding Father, revealed his view of woman's role in society. He suggested that women should avoid any activity that would require deep thinking and should avoid novels and much of the poetry of the period, which he felt would pollute their minds. Female education should concentrate, he said, on "ornaments and the amusements of life," which, he felt, were "dancing, drawing and music."[6]

Those women who dared to stray from the norm were often publicly reprimanded, even punished, and in some communities were branded as witches. Women in most states were not allowed to own property, did not pay taxes, and could not sit as jurors or hold elective offices. They were banned from medical schools and law schools, and although there were women's colleges in the mid-1800s, most functioned as finishing schools at best.

In 1868, there had been a moment of hope. When women learned that a constitutional amendment enfranchising all Americans, regardless of race, color, or creed had been passed, suffragists felt that women would no longer be treated as second-class citizens. But their joy was quickly defused when they learned that the amendment had not been designed with women in mind. It had been intended to provide male ex-slaves with full citizenship and all of the rights and privileges that go with that citizenship. Only in 1920, after many years of organized campaigning and protesting, did American women finally win the right to vote.

The Continuing Struggle

While American women today hold elective offices, practice medicine and law, attend Harvard and Yale, and head corporations, they have had to sacrifice much to make it in a "man's world." These accomplishments have required them to recognize and master the male traits that are needed to succeed in a patriarchal society. Doing so has also required them to suppress other, more feminine qualities such as gentleness and compassion.

While more and more women compete in the male-dominated professional world, they are falling victim to many of the same stress-related diseases that have long afflicted men. The rate of heart attacks among women has increased substantially, as has the suicide rate.[7]

While some women seem to be trying to outdo men by being more "masculine," there is also a traditionalist element of women who remain captives of the dehumanizing myths, which they embrace as divinely ordained truths. The vast majority of women seem to be straddling the two opposing extremes. While they sense the need for the advancement of women and will applaud those advancements that are made, they remain fearful of giving up the pattern of life to which they have become accustomed. To survive, they have been forced to adjust to certain social aspects of an unjust world; and one of those aspects is the established female role.

Women's efforts to seek equal opportunities have been the cause of confusion and anger among many males. Unaccustomed to warding off challenges from elements of society whom they believe to be beneath them, many men resent assertive women, whom they characterize as "pushy." Unable to grasp that the message behind female assertiveness is a cry for social justice, these men work hard to keep women in their "rightful place." While the majority of men are trying to make the best of an escalating and unsettling social condition, a few men are sincerely trying to aid the women's rights cause, much like Frederick Douglass did in his time.

The ex-slave turned abolitionist was not only an avid fighter of slavery and racism, he was passionate about women winning equal status with men as well. Douglass urged the leadership of the American women's rights movement to petition the government for the right to vote. He was the only man to address the first women's rights convention, held in Seneca Falls, New York, in 1848. Elizabeth Cady Stanton, the leading organizer of the convention, as well as other leaders of the movement, were impressed with Douglass's sincere dedication to their cause. It is easy to understand why they were impressed, for Douglass combined moral sensitivity and compassion—qualities usually considered feminine—with his traditionally masculine skills as a powerful orator, journalist, and courageous advocate of human rights. Stanton, it should be noted, displayed powers of abstraction and visionary leadership—attributes normally thought to be the exclusive domain of men.

The advancement of women will not be realized until the great majority of men own the issue. By that is meant that each man must recognize his own deep-rooted sense of superiority toward women, must conscientiously work to overcome it, and must wholeheartedly work for the equality of women and men. This can be done in the workplace, the school one attends, and the clubs one belongs to, by ensuring that qualified women are chosen to hold responsible positions, by encouraging girls to pursue careers traditionally reserved for men, by tutoring girls in mathematics and science, by supporting qualified female candidates for the local school board, by frequenting female-owned businesses, by volunteering to baby-sit, cook meals, and wash dishes at home and at community events, and by becoming a public advocate of women's rights.

Of course, men cannot secure equal rights for women all by themselves. Women who are fearful of "rocking the boat"—and they are the great majority of women—need to be helped to see that they have been brainwashed into thinking they are inferior. They need to work actively to overcome that spirit-crippling attitude so that they can be free to develop to their full potential. As mothers, they need to be aware that they have the all-important responsibility of inculcating in their children—both male and female—that the oneness of humankind includes the equality of the sexes, that unity of the human family is unattainable if half of the world's population continues to struggle to attain equal status with men.

Basic Gender Differences

To inculcate this principle, both mother and father need to understand that, though males and females are both human beings, they have different basic functions. This does not make one sex superior to the other. The differences relate to their different physical makeups. It stands to reason that the mother, who carries and delivers a baby and breast-feeds the child, is going to be more nurturing and patient than the father. At the same time, the father is likely to show more assertiveness in finding ways to ensure the security of his wife and child. This pattern has become the basis for much of our current thinking of men as task-oriented and of women as more emotional and expressive.

The qualities and attributes that each gender has to offer in relationships and enterprises are necessary to creating a harmonious society. The trouble is that most men and women are not aware that we all possess the same latent spiritual qualities. Each sex has the tendency to emphasize different qualities, due, in part, to childbearing and rearing responsibilities. What usually happens is that those qualities end up shaping and dominating our attitudinal and behavioral patterns, while the other qualities remain under-developed. Balance is required. On the one hand, men need to learn to rely on intuition more and become more gentle, patient, and nurturing—qualities that are generally far more developed among women. On the other hand, women need to become more forthright, assertive, and analytical—qualities that are generally far more developed among men.

Obviously, a balance of all of these qualities is required in developing just and harmonious relationships. Ideally, men must learn to appreciate female values and recognize how they can benefit men and the community-at-large. When that happens, men will very likely adopt such values and manifest them as needed. At the same time, women will find it useful to develop certain male values and learn to use them in making their mark in the world.

Again, balance is the key. This need for balance is eloquently summarized by the late Bahá'í leader 'Abdu'l-Bahá in a talk given while touring America in 1912:

The world of humanity is possessed of two wings: the male and the female. So long as these two wings are not equivalent in strength, the bird will not fly. Until womankind reaches the same degree as man, until she enjoys the same arena of activity, extraordinary attainment for humanity will not be realized; humanity cannot wing its way to heights of real attainment. When the two wings . . . become equivalent in strength, enjoying the same prerogatives, the flight of man will be exceedingly lofty and extraordinary.[9]

CHAPTER 6

A NEW PERSPECTIVE ON WHO WE ARE AND WHERE WE LIVE

Let us proceed as if the myth of female inferiority and the other myths mentioned in previous chapters were nonexistent and try to describe the structure of humanity and its place in creation. We will first establish our place in creation, because knowing our place in the grand scheme of things will help us to determine how we should behave.

Our Place in the Universe

Though we are accustomed to locating ourselves in terms of country, state, city, and street, this is only part of the picture. If we widen our vision, we realize that we are inhabitants of the planet Earth, which is only one tiny planet in a single galaxy, which is only a small one among countless galaxies. In reality, our planet is one tiny part of a systematic whole—the universe—that is so immense it is beyond anyone's capacity to measure it. Considering the immensity of the universe, our planet is practically invisible in relation to all of creation. It is like a dynamic microscopic cell in a boundless body that is in constant motion and changes unceasingly.

Astronomers are now beginning to think of the universe as an ongoing dramatic event. According to quantum theory, matter is always restless, never static. This is true of the imperceptible elements of reality such as subatomic particles, atoms, molecules, cells, and innumerable bacteria living everywhere, in every nook and cranny of our planet. In every human mouth, for example, there are more bacteria than there are people on our planet.[1] Even in inorganic objects such as a piece of furniture there are interconnected pockets of energy.

Just as the universe is in constant motion, so is our planet. The Earth is turning so rapidly that we do not notice its spinning; nor are we able to sense its continuous journey around our star, the Sun. Each revolution of this unending journey, which we fully trust will never stop, takes 365 and one-quarter days to complete. Each orbit that the spaceship Earth makes around the Sun constitutes a year. But it isn't as if our planet is zipping around a motionless star. The Sun is moving too. In effect, it is as if Earth and all of the other planets in our solar system were piggybacking on the Sun as it traverses our galaxy. The Sun has circled our galaxy eighteen times in the approximately fifteen billion years that Earth has existed.

Though it is not apparent to the naked eye, change is constant throughout all of creation. The only thing that does not change is change itself. Change is occurring everywhere, from the vast expanses of outer space to every cell, molecule, and atom within our bodies. For example, 98 percent of the atoms in our body were not there three months ago. Every month we have a "new" skin. We have a new stomach lining every four days. And every six weeks we have a new liver. Even within the brain, its basic chemical composition fluctuates. For example, the brain's content of carbon, nitrogen, oxygen, and so on is totally different today than it was a year ago. As endocrinologist Deepak Chopra explains,

> It is as if you lived in a building whose bricks were systematically taken out and replaced each year. If you keep the same blue print, then it will still look like the same building. But it won't be the same in actuality. The human body also stands there looking much the same from day to day, but through the processes of respiration, digestion, elimination, and so forth, it is constantly and ever in exchange with the rest of the world.[1]

So it is safe to say that biologically we are not the same as we were the year before, and next year we will be different than we are this year.

There is so much going on all around us that we cannot see which affects us on a regular basis. Gravity, electricity, magnetism, and nuclear energy are unobservable forces that affect us constantly. We know they exist only because we are able to discern their effects on ourselves and the world around us. For example, the person who tumbles from a roof and lives to tell about the fall has experienced the effect of gravity. Just as there are planetary invisible realities such as gravity, there is a Universal, invisible Reality. This Universal Reality not only affects the orchestration of the universe and all of its intricacies and complexities, it can also affect human beings in a positive way if they choose to partake of the love and knowledge streaming from this Unknowable Essence, which the religious call "the Creator," or "God."

Our planet is in the galaxy known as the Milky Way. There are hundreds of billions of stars and planets in the Milky Way, most of them much bigger than our star and our planet. To put the Earth's size into perspective in relation to the rest of creation, consider this: If the Milky Way galaxy were to be reduced to the size of Earth, our planet would vanish into a particle of dust that would be too small to see.[2]

Of course, there are countless galaxies. And within each of these galaxies there are hundreds of billions of stars and planets, each in some stage of development or decline. No wonder Earth is invisible to all of creation! While our galaxy is considered to be among the smallest, to us it is immense. To travel from one end to another at the speed of light (186,000 miles per second) would take 120,000 years. Contrary to the beliefs of renowned ancient theologians and philosophers, the Earth is not the center of the universe; nor is our solar system the center of our galaxy. In fact, it is actually on the edge of our galaxy, in its "suburbs."

As we gaze at the stars, knowing there is so much more than we can see, we cannot help being struck with awe at the inexplicable immensity and complexity of the structure before and beyond us. It is a humbling experience, because in the context of boundless space, we seem insignificant.

What a wonder is evolving creation! All of the galaxies with their myriad heavenly bodies, and on Earth millions of animal and plant species, on land and in the sea, functioning in a pattern perfectly suited to their environment. Operating flawlessly, their essence remains a marvelous mystery. To believe that such a creation came about through a series of accidents is akin to believing that the *Encyclopaedia Britannica* is the result of an explosion in a printing press.

"Today," physicist Fritjof Capra states, "the universe is no longer seen [by some scientists] as a machine, made up of a multitude of separate objects, but appears as a harmonious indivisible whole; a network of dynamic relationships that include the human observer and his or her consciousness in an essential way."[3] Physicist James Jeans senses that the universe is a spiritual entity: "Today there is a wide measure of agreement . . . that the stream of knowledge is heading towards a non-mechanical reality; the universe begins to look more like a great thought than a giant machine."[4]

Despite the complexity and awesome vastness of the field of countless pulsating galaxies, it pales in comparison to the wondrousness of a single human soul, brain, and nervous system. Those unique features of a human being are capable of acknowledging the existence of the universe and making strides through invention in understanding its operation and function, as well as identifying its resources and developing them for the benefit of humankind. No galaxy, regardless of size and splendor, can do that. Human creativity, intelligence, intuition, and spirituality are unique in creation.

The continually moving and changing microscopic speck that we think of as Earth is not a stationary round rock that simply houses life. In a sense, it functions as a womb from which life is produced by its soil, which is full of nutrients that produce trees, grasses, flowers, fruits, and vegetables that help to sustain animals and humans. A delicate chemical balance exists on Earth that is necessary to maintaining life. For eons the oxygen content of the atmosphere has been maintained at 21 percent. A few percent more, and all vegetation would burn. Geological evidence indicates that Earth's oceans have contained 3.4 percent salt for thousands of years. Were the concentration of salt to rise by a mere 2.5 percent, life in the ocean would come to an end. Without the ozone layer of the upper atmosphere, all life on Earth would be annihilated. This extraordinary balance is also evident in the human body. Despite exposure to extreme temperatures, humans' internal temperatures seldom vary by more than a degree or two. For the most part, the human body temperature stays at 98.6 degrees Fahrenheit.[5]

The Oneness of Life

Our planet can be thought of as a sensitive, living organism teeming with humans and all other forms of life, which are continually interacting either directly or indirectly. There is an interconnection between all levels of creation. Physicist Fritjof Capra describes this interconnection in the book *Turningpoint,* explaining what makes our planet a living organism:

> All the living matter on Earth, together with the atmosphere, oceans and soil, forms a complex system that has all the characteristic patterns of self-organization. It persists in a remarkable state of chemical and thermodynamic nonequilibrium and is able, through a huge variety of processes, to regulate the planetary environment so that optimal conditions for the evolution of life are maintained.
>
> For example, the climate on Earth has never been totally unfavorable for life since living forms first appeared, about four billion years ago. During that long period of time the radiation from the Sun increased by at least 30 percent. If the earth were simply a solid inanimate object, its surface temperature would follow the Sun's energy output, which means that the whole Earth would have been a frozen sphere for more than a billion years. We know from geological records that such adverse conditions never existed. The planet maintained a fairly constant surface temperature throughout the evolution of life, much as a human organism maintains a constant body temperature in spite of varying environmental conditions.

Similar patterns of self-regulation can be observed for other environmental properties, such as the chemical composition of the atmosphere, the salt content of the oceans, and the distribution of trace elements among plants and animals. All of these are regulated by intricate cooperative networks that exhibit the properties of self-organizing systems. The earth then, is a living system; it functions not just like an organism, but actually seems to be an organism—Gaia, a living planetary being. Her properties and activities cannot be predicted from the sum of her parts; every one of her tissues is linked to every other tissue and all of them are mutually interdependent; her many pathways of communication are highly complex and nonlinear; her form has evolved over billions of years and continues to evolve. These observations were made within a scientific context, but they go far beyond science. Like many other aspects of their new paradigm, they reflect a profound ecological awareness that is ultimately spiritual.[6]

It took me years to understand that the millions of species comprising life on Earth are fluctuating aspects, or focal points, of a single living organism, and that life exists in places not noticeable to the human eye. For example, within our atmosphere there is invisible life. A shovel full of soil contains a microbe population greater than that of humankind.[7] The human being ends up absorbing many of the microbes in the Earth's soil by eating the vegetables and fruits grown in the soil. Even meat eaters absorb soil-bound microbes through cattle, sheep, pigs, and chickens that graze on grasses and consume animal feed.

The building blocks of life are everywhere. Even in seemingly empty places. For example, every cubic centimeter of air contains some ten billion, billion molecules.[8] With every breath that we inhale, we are ingesting innumerable molecules that once existed in people of the past and present, as well as in other organisms on the planet.

Yes, all that exists is interrelated, even in the invisible realm. Electricity and magnetism, once believed by physicists to be separate forces of nature, manifest an underlying oneness: A changing magnetic field creates an electric field, and vice versa, so that both are now regarded as aspects of a single force field, the electromagnetic field. In the visible realm, we eat, drink, and breathe the Earth—and also the Sun and the Milky Way and the universe. For are not bread, and meat, and rain part of the Earth? And is not the Earth part of the Sun, and the Sun part of the Milky Way, and all of them part of the universe? In the book *Being Peace,* Buddhist philosopher Thich Nhat Hanh offers a wonderful explanation of interrelatedness, or oneness:

Just as a piece of paper is the fruit, the combination of many elements that can be called non-paper elements, the individual is made of non-individual elements. If you are a poet, you will see clearly that there is a cloud floating in this sheet of paper. Without a cloud there will be no water; without water, the trees cannot grow; and without trees, you cannot make paper. So the cloud is in here. The existence of this page is dependent on the existence of the cloud. Paper and cloud is so close. Let us think of other things, like the sunshine. Sunshine is very important because the forest cannot grow without sunshine. So the logger needs sunshine in order to cut the tree, and the tree needs the sunshine in order to be a tree. Therefore you can see sunshine in this sheet of paper. And if you look more deeply . . . with the eyes of those who are awake, you see not only the cloud and the sunshine in it, but that everything is here: the wheat that became the bread for the logger to eat, the logger's father—everything is in this sheet of paper.[9]

Like Thich Nhat Hanh, naturalist John Muir, who spent a lifetime observing facets of life, saw the interrelatedness of all things. "When we try to pick out anything by itself," he wrote, "we find it hitched to everything else in the universe."[10]

The Oneness of Humanity and Unity in Diversity

Because humanity is part of the universe, it is therefore interconnected, despite some people's protests to the contrary. The millions of known species on Earth are all aspects of a single reality. The human aspect is a species we call Homo sapiens sapiens. While all species have different capacities and functions, they all share some similar qualities. For example, the power of attraction, which keeps the atoms of a rock together, also exists in humans; a plant, like the rock, possesses the power of attraction, plus the powers of growth and reproduction, which are also evident in humans; an animal contains the qualities of the rock and the plant as well as sensory powers and consciousness, which we all possess. The quality that distinguishes humans from animals is the power of ideation—the ability to be conscious of our consciousness and our spiritual dimension. All Homo sapiens sapiens—that is, all human beings—are, in reality, members of one family, regardless of skin color, culture, geographical location, facial features, texture of hair, language or ethnicity. This is a fact despite all attempts to proclaim otherwise.

In connection with this reality, paleontologist Richard Leakey puts the oneness of humankind in sharp perspective:

> We are one species, one people. Every individual on this earth is a member of Homo sapiens sapiens, and the geographical variations we see among peoples are simply biological nuances on the basic theme.

The human capacity for culture permits its elaboration in widely different and colorful ways. The often very deep differences between those cultures should be interpreted for what they really are: the ultimate declaration of belonging to the human species.[11]

It is difficult for some people to accept the idea that everyone in the world is related. To embrace the idea is to go against the grain of most people's lifelong conditioning. It means giving up part of our belief system, which is familiar and provides a degree of security and comfort. In fact, the thought of being related to people living in different lands, or for that matter to different people in our own land, who seem strange and threatening, is, for some, beyond comprehension and perhaps even revolting. It is a basic human instinct to want to be with people who look like us, eat the same kinds of foods we eat, practice the same religion we do, enjoy the same kind of music we like. Familiarity is comforting, but it also has a way of generating a sense of community pride that can, in time, evolve into a deep-seated prejudice and a sense of superiority toward all who are different from those with whom we are most comfortable. Such prejudices are not usually born out of malice, but rather from the fear of giving up a way of life and certain privileges to which we have become accustomed. Change, which is a natural phenomenon, is viewed with suspicion. We are willing to be tolerant of those we find strange and inferior as long as we don't have to interact with them. Because we fear the present and distrust the future, we embrace the past.

Nevertheless, time passes and human progress does not stop. In the past 150 years there have been remarkable technological breakthroughs: Medical advances are allowing us to live longer; infantile deaths have been sharply reduced; cures for diseases once thought incurable have been discovered; a collective social awareness has developed, drawing nations together in efforts to alleviate famine and rescue of victims of manmade or natural disasters; collective efforts to overcome poverty are on the increase. All of these changes and more are factors in the rapid growth of our planet's population. With advances in transportation and the emergence of a global economy, more people from different parts of the world are working together and living in the same neighborhoods. Yet many of these people still harbor age-old prejudices toward those with whom they are forced to live and work.

This process of population growth and involuntary social integration, which is accelerating at a phenomenal rate, will result either in community disaster or harmony. If the prejudices are not overcome, they can explode into aggressive bigotry, for if there is no sincere or compassionate appreciation of one another's differences, then those differences will represent a threat to the beholder's way of life. One who is thus ruled by ignorance, arrogance, and fear will treat his neighbor as a dangerous enemy. When such attitudes are widespread, we have the potential makings of the situations in Bosnia, Rwanda, or Kosovo.

If, however, neighbors representing different ethnicities make a genuine effort to understand and appreciate one another's differences, then a meaningful step will be made in the development of a harmonious community. This can be done if all parties become acquainted with and internalize the interrelated principles of the oneness of humankind and unity in diversity. Actually, unity in diversity becomes apparent when oneness is embraced. A person realizes that, despite all of the differences in the world, all people stem from the same source. While people maintain their own individuality, they share the same root system. An example of unity in diversity in nature:

the fruit, blossoms, leaves, twigs, branches, and trunk, which make up a tree, receive their sustenance from the same set of roots. Every living tree's different parts are unified.

It is important to keep in mind that these principles are not mere concepts, nor are they simply the wishful thinking of well-meaning optimists. They are not the result of some sudden development in evolution or the recent revelation of a modern seer. These principles have always existed, as real as gravity and Earth's continual movement around the Sun. That prehistoric cave dwellers and the early champions of Western Enlightenment were not aware of them does not mean these principles were not in operation. They were always in existence, waiting to be discovered and put into practice.

Practicing the Oneness of Humanity and Unity in Diversity

Putting the principles of the oneness of humanity and unity in diversity into practice is not an easy undertaking, considering what it can take to unravel the emotional attachment to ignorance. The first impulse is often to ignore the challenge through various rationalizations such as "It will take too much time and cause too much pain." Giving up what is familiar and trusted in favor of an unfamiliar condition would be another excuse. No doubt, trying to make the adjustment to change is stressful.

Nonetheless, despite the difficulty of the challenge, it must be met. Furthermore, the challenge cannot be met halfheartedly. It must be met with persistence, enthusiasm, and determination—in short, with the passion of a pioneering trailblazer. To reject the challenge is like rejecting electricity because one was brought up using oil lamps. It is tantamount to allowing falsehood to prevail over truth. But there is an even more profound reason for meeting the challenge: Humanity's survival and the establishment of true world peace depend on it.

Should the great majority of humans recognize and sincerely involve themselves in practicing these two principles, most of the intercultural rivalries and animosities that keep the human family splintered, wrapt in suspicion and on the edge of violence, would vanish. People would begin to notice and appreciate their basic similarities as well as their superficial differences. They would focus on one another's good qualities and would avoid dwelling on each other's faults. There would be a collective awareness of how foolish and costly it is to adhere to beliefs that prevent us from recognizing the oneness of the human family. Liberated from an ancient ignorance that has bred long-lasting hatreds, people would engage in a universal celebration of oneness that would become the secure foundation of a lasting peace in our war-weary world. To realize this achievable scenario, however, men and women must have the knowledge that will inspire them to transcend their social conditioning and embrace, once and for all, the truth of which their ancestors were unaware.

In his book titled *The Seven Mysteries of Life*, noted science writer Guy Murchie explains what makes the familyhood of all humankind a reality:

> . . . no human being (of any race) can be less closely related to any other human than approximately fiftieth cousin, and most of us (no matter what color our neighbors) are a lot closer. Indeed this low magnitude for the lineal compass of mankind is accepted by the leading geneticists I have consulted (from J. B. S. Haldane to Theodosius Dobzhansky to Sir Julian Huxley), and it means simply that the family trees of all of us, of whatsoever origin or trait, must meet and merge into one genetic tree of all humanity by the time they have

soared into our ancestries for about fifty generations. This is not a particularly abstruse fact, for simple arithmetic demonstrates that, if we double the number of our ancestors for each generation as we reckon backward (consistently multiplying them by two: 2 parents, 4 grand-parents, 8 great grandparents, 16 great, great grandparents, etc.), our personal pedigrees would cover mankind before the thirtieth genera-tion. Mathematics is quite explosive in that regard, you see, for the thirtieth power of two (1,073,741,824) turns out to be much larger than was the earth's population thirty generations ago—that is, in the thirteenth century if we assume 25 years to a generation.

But you cannot reasonably go on doubling your ancestors for more than a very few generations into the past because inevitably the same ancestor will appear on both your father's and your mother's sides of your family tree, reducing the total number (since you can't count the same person twice), and this must happen more and more as you go back in time. The basic reason it happens is that spouses are not just spouses but they are also cousins (although the relationship is usually too distant to be noticed), which means they are related to each other not only by marriage but also by "blood" because somewhere in the past they share ancestors. Another way of saying it is that your father's family tree and your mother's inevitably overlap, intertwine and be-come one tree as their generations branch out backward, a process forced by geometry until eventually all your ancestors are playing double, triple, quadruple and higher-multiple roles as both, all quar-ters, eighths, etc. . . . of your tree finally merge with others into one common whole and the broad tops of the family trees of everyone alive and his family become identical with their ancestral world popu-lations. These populations of course are the fertile portions of past societies and naturally cannot include "old maids," cautious bachelors or anyone who fails to beget at least one continuous line of fecund descendants to disseminate his genes into mankind's future.[12]

Thus the genetic linkage between all humans is strong. But the biological linkage goes beyond genetics. There is an invisible biological chain that links all human beings, as well as all of the animal species on our planet. It is called breathing. It is estimated that we take approximately 30,000 breaths daily.[13] In a year's time we take about 10,800,000 breaths. Every time we inhale we take in trillions of atoms, and every time we exhale we release trillions of atoms. We know that without atoms we cannot have molecules; without molecules we cannot have cells; without cells we cannot have tissues; without tissues we cannot have organs; and without organs we cannot have human beings. So every time we exhale we release bits and pieces of heart cells, brain cells, liver cells, DNA, and so on, all of which is taken in by those around us regardless of skin-color, culture, education, religion, or occupation. When we inhale we are taking in infinitesimally small bits and pieces of the tissues, organs, and DNA of those around us. When we are outdoors, the wind takes what we have exhaled to different parts of the world, where they are inhaled and absorbed by other people.

In this way, the person who hates people of a certain color may well possess particles of cells that were once a part of those he hates. This interchange of bits and pieces of cells has been going on ever since the dawn of life on Earth. It becomes easy to see that the idea of a "pure" race has always been a groundless assumption, nothing more than pure fantasy.

Perhaps the greatest proof that all humans belong to the same species, or family, is seen when an interracial couple produces a child. There are people who believe that Africans, Asians, Europeans, American Indians, Hispanics are different species, just as dogs, rats, and cats are different species. Obviously, this warped notion about the human family is disproved every time an interracial couple produces a child, for two different species cannot produce a viable offspring.

While all things are interrelated, every living thing is different. This paradoxical aspect of reality manifests itself in the principle of unity in diversity. In nature, no two things are exactly alike, yet they all stem from the same reality. Every cell in our body is unique, as is each snowflake, each rose, even roses of the same color. Within a litter of puppies, each puppy has its own temperament, coloring, and size. No two human beings, including identical twins, have identical fingerprints. Though all four of my children are different, they are linked through the same roots, much like a tree. None of a tree's branches, twigs, leaves, blossoms, or fruits are exactly alike, yet they are part of a whole, tied to one set of roots, which are tied to the soil and the Sun, which supply their nutrients.

One of the best illustrations of this principle of unity in diversity can be seen in the structure of the human body. Though the heart, lungs, pancreas, liver, stomach, and kidneys all have different functions, they must operate harmoniously if the body is to manifest good health. They are the essential parts that make up the whole. In and of itself, none of these parts has any real value, but together they have a purpose.

The very existence of such differences suggests that our Creator loves variety as well as unity. Our Creator has provided a beautiful base for us to build on, a backdrop that will soothe the spirit. Through the principle of unity in diversity we are given an example of how to live in harmony and balance, as do the lower orders of life. But beyond that, the principle motivates humans to create civilizations that will continually advance materially and spiritually. If everyone were to look alike, think alike, feel alike, dress alike, eat alike, and live in houses that are the same, there would be no incentive for people to better their community's condition, to explore the universe's rich resources in order to create mechanisms and programs that would improve the quality of life on Earth.

The principle of unity in diversity is exemplified in a truly harmonious marriage. Though man and woman stem from essentially the same source, they possess different emotional and physical impulses that are necessary to carrying out certain natural functions. The woman is designed to carry an embryo and deliver a human being into this world and nourish it with her own milk. To help her carry out her motherly responsibilities, she is endowed with a more passive, caring nature, and she relies more on intuition in making decisions than her husband does. While she, on the one hand, tends to be more process oriented, he is more product oriented. She tends to seek to maintain social relationships within her home and elsewhere. Her husband, on the other hand, tends to be more achievement driven, more aggressive than his wife. This instinct is used to provide his family with the necessities of life. When confronted with a social problem, his desire is to solve it immediately, while the wife wants to determine the cause of the problem and consider different points of view before attempting to devise a solution. This description of the differing natures of men and women is not meant to belittle one and commend the other. Both are of equal value, for both serve the purpose of ensuring familial survival. In the successful and harmonious marriage, husband and wife are aware of, and respect one another's different natures and appreciate their purpose. In such a relationship, the wife becomes more assertive and independent, and the husband becomes more caring, more relationship centered, less aggressive. When there is a blending of masculine and feminine qualities, the marital union is strengthened.

The same kind of harmony can be achieved in a community composed of different ethnic groups. When there is appreciation for others' positive attributes and material contributions, there is a tendency to want to embrace those qualities. Italians now eat bagels, and Jews eat pizza. Obviously, sincere and regular intercultural exchanges can bring about more substantive, more unific results.

"The diversity in the human family," said 'Abdu'l-Bahá, "should be the cause of love and harmony, as it is in music where many different notes blend together in the making of a perfect chord."[14]

Understanding Our Diversity

While diversity beautifies nature and serves as a catalyst for human development, it also has a practical biological side. One practical example can be seen in differences of skin pigmentation. While every human being has the pigment melanin, those living in hot, sunny climates have more of it, which darkens the skin, shielding it from the cancer-producing rays of the tropical sun. Another practical example can be seen in the development of the sickle cell. In heavily forested, hot, humid places in Africa, where the risk of infection with malaria is great, the indigenous people have, over time, developed the sickle cell (crescent-shaped red blood cell) in their blood systems, providing them with immunity to falciparum malaria.[15]

It is true that people living in different parts of the world have different values and may, therefore, behave differently. When we are unaware of the reasons for these differences, we tend to develop prejudicial thoughts and behaviors. However, there are commonsense reasons for the differences, which have little to do with genetic makeup. Modern science points out that environment affects how genes work; thus environment is the key to the development of basic values.[16]

For example, there are environmental factors that explain why northern Europeans tend to be linear, hierarchical, and dichotomous in their thinking; why they have a propensity for precision, planning, and promptness; and why they tend to be object centered and aggressive. These values originated thousands of years ago, when human life expectancy was half of what it is today. There were no refrigerators, freezers, stoves, heaters, or air conditioners. Life was harsh because the terrain was rugged, the climate severe, and the means of transportation and communication primitive. Survival was the primary aim of existence. Faced with a short growing season, people were forced to plan precisely when and how to plant and when to harvest. If they failed to do so, they would die. As a result, counting and measuring accurately became very important to the northern Europeans. They became very conservation conscious as well, because they had to make sure that they had enough food to last throughout the year. Fighting the elements and making sure that no one would steal their food encouraged aggression; thus they built forts to protect what they had grown and stored. Those who built the forts needed men whom they could trust to defend the storehouses; the institution of knighthood was created, leading to the development of a hierarchical system that is still reflected in today's business, educational, political, and religious communities throughout northern Europe and those places to which northern Europeans migrated. With so much energy focused on time quick decision making, northern Europeans did not have much opportunity to think cosmically. As a consequence, they developed the tendency to focus on the parts to understand the whole. There was little time to explore different aspects of a conflict, for they needed to be able to quickly judge issues and people as either right or wrong, good or bad.

By contrast, west Africans tend to be nonlinear and intuitive in their thinking, being less preoccupied with objects and more concerned with relationships and having a flexible view of time. By focusing on the whole, they gain an understanding of the parts. These values, like those of the northern Europeans, were born thousands of years ago out of the need to survive under a particular set of circumstances. Living in an environment where there is a limitless growing period, west Africans were able to develop a flexible view of time. There was no need to store and hoard food, no need to build forts, no need to rush.

West Africans have consequently learned to look upon all of the people of their village as family members and to share willingly what they have with others. There are no orphanages, because every child is viewed as one's own. So a west African's home is not his house; the whole village is his home. There is no need to call ahead if you wish to visit with a friend. Not feeling pressured by time, a west African will explore every aspect of an issue and rely on intuition to make a decision. Unlike the northern European, the west African's learning style is based on symbolic imagery and rhythm. This, because the major means of communication for west Africans was dance and song.

Because of two hundred years of racial discrimination and segregation, Americans of west African heritage possess, for the most part, their ancestors' learning style. Living in predominantly Black neighborhoods, they have had relatively few opportunities for meaningful interaction with the northern Europeans who seized control of America. They were forced, by and large, to adopt and practice the values of their ethnic ancestors. Portland, Oregon, educator Joy Leary has studied the way urban African-American students learn, finding that they react positively to story-telling and the "rap" form of communication, which is based on rhythm. She discovered that the Black ghetto child finds it easier and more pleasurable to create and memorize a fifteen-minute rap than to learn how to spell a list of words.

Developing a World Culture

The fact that ethnic values have existed for many years does not mean that they will continue to exist as they are today. They will change, and more quickly than we think, because of rapidly accelerating technological advances and because of the growing number of interracial marriages that are fostering a worldwide global consciousness.

Whether we realize it or not, we are in the process of developing a world culture. Never before have so many people migrated from one continent to another. Second-generation Americans whose parents came from Nigeria, Japan, or Peru have integrated into American society and are adopting values that may seem foreign to their parents. They also contribute, in a small way, some of their ancestral cultural characteristics to the forever changing cultural tapestry that is America. This is exemplified in the way that many young Americans greet each other these days. It is practically a dance, reminiscent of the way west Africans usually greet one another. Through the wonder of global television, youth in other countries are adopting the greeting ritual. People are high-fiving in Ireland, Colombia, Russia, and Japan.

Though there will be an even greater blending of values in the future, diversity will always exist within the human family, but not along racial lines. The differences will be centered on personality traits, character development, vocational interests and talents, human potentialities, creativity, and intellectual attainment.

While human differences are natural, oneness and unity are equally natural. If we accept differences and ignore oneness, which is the reality from which all differences stem, we help to perpetuate the strife that afflicts our human family, and we reinforce the apartheid rooted in our communities. Blacks and Whites rarely interact socially after work hours on a regular basis; the same is true of Christians and Jews, Hispanics and Anglos. Most American Indians are segregated by design or choice, as are most Asian Americans. As long as this condition persists, ethnic groups will continue to avoid, as much as possible, interaction with each other. Within such an unnatural social climate, prejudices bloom and abound. When we avoid intercultural interaction, our perception of other ethnic groups is usually fashioned by our parents' distorted views and our community's collective feelings toward other ethnic groups—which generally are not based on fact but on ignorance and fear.

Because the reality of oneness, or interrelatedness, is so foreign to most of us, we doubt and even reject its existence. By doing so, we turn our backs on a fundamental principle of life. In some respects, this is like ignoring or rejecting the existence of the Sun. The oneness of humankind is a vital and essential aspect of God's grand design—so much so that He considers all people His children. Therefore, for the collective good of humanity, this principle needs to be recognized, understood, and internalized. True world peace hinges on its universal acceptance, for the establishment of peace and unity must be based on a sense of familyhood between peoples and na-tions. But that kind of unity cannot be achieved simply through conflict resolution, political treaties, or pious and wishful thinking. When we un-derstand human nature and the purpose of life, it is easier to understand and put into practice the principle of the oneness of humankind. The difference between oneness and unity becomes clear.

Oneness is a principle, a fundamental truth. Unity is a process. No one is going to establish the oneness of the human family; our Creator has already taken care of that. The trouble is that the human family is not yet united. One of the reasons it isn't united is because we are ignorant of our oneness. Trying to create unity without internalizing oneness will prove to be a futile exercise. Many well-meaning people have tried to unify their communities without embracing this principle and have met with frustration and failure. After repeatedly failing in their attempts, many people have given up trying, feeling doubt and a sense of hopelessness. Some stoics continue the effort through periodic race-unity picnics and parades, which rarely produce the desired results.

While oneness and unity are different, they are closely related. The mechanics of unity are inherent in oneness, just as the mechanics of an oak tree are inherent in an acorn. Should an acorn be properly nourished, it will evolve into an oak tree. Deprived of nourishment, the acorn will not fulfill its destiny. When we internalize oneness, the latent unifying energy within us is activated, and we become a force for unity in our community, in our home, and in our workplace. A pleasant urge to bring people together encompasses our entire being. Success in unifying people—all kinds of people—brings us great joy. It is such a wonderful feeling that we seek opportunities to unite people wherever we may be.

Everyone, regardless of education, culture, economic status, language, vocation, or skin color, has the potential to be a force for unity in his or her community. But realizing that potential requires that we internalize the oneness of humankind. Fully understanding our spiritual reality and realizing that all humans are closer than fiftieth cousins helps us to internalize this principal. We realize that, spiritually, we are brothers and sisters. How is this so?

The soul is a spiritual emanation from God. That means all of the nearly six billion human souls on our planet are connected to God, just as a ray of sunlight is connected to the Sun. Because we are all connected to God, that makes God our true mother and father. Sharing the same mother and father makes everyone we know—as well as everyone we don't know, everyone we like or dislike, trust or distrust, love or hate—our spiritual brothers and sisters. With such an awareness, how can we not view our fellow human beings with greater compassion and willingness to set aside our grudges and suspicions? A desire to help each other will naturally replace the tendency to look out for one's own interests first, and the natural instinct to love and protect members of our nuclear family will be extended to the members of our greater human family. When that happens, the present planetary condition of hopelessness, fear, and selfishness will give way to hope, optimism, joy, and a sincere, energetic desire to help turn our planet into what it was meant to be—a haven of love and justice.

We know that this is possible, because when disasters such as hurricanes, earthquakes, tornadoes, or floods strike a community, the instinct to love and protect is extended to strangers, regardless of color, religion, or ethnicity—even to long-time enemies. Rich and poor; Black and White; Christian, Jew, Muslim, Buddhist, and Hindu help each other to look for survivors, repair homes, and bury the dead. During a physical crisis of great magnitude prejudice disappears, and unity is practiced. The imaginary barriers that keep people apart are washed away along with the roads, bridges, and houses.

This same dynamic often holds true on the battlefield. When Black and White soldiers, who normally would have nothing to do with one another, are huddled together in a trench, they are united in thought and purpose and are willing to help each other survive. The social barriers that once kept them apart no longer exist. Through genuine cooperation in times of need, we learn to care for each other, and in time true unity follows. We find ourselves operating as a family is meant to operate.

In an open letter to the world's children, United Nations Secretary-General Kofi Annan gives an example of how our inherent instinct to love and protect our fellow human beings is manifested:

> Computers and modems help us talk and listen to each other across the world. But that wouldn't do us much good if we didn't already have a lot in common. And we do. We may have different religions, different languages, different colored skins, but we all belong to one human race. We all share the same basic values.
>
> Imagine for a moment that you saw a smaller child run in front of a bus approaching at full speed. What would you do? You wouldn't stop and think. You'd rush to save the child—even though that meant putting yourself in danger. You'd be a hero. Except that you don't have to be a hero to act like that. It's human instinct.[17]

Though the UN Secretary-General is a believer in the oneness of humankind, most of humanity does not share his belief. If they did, the world would be in better shape. Unfortunately, many influential institutions that were designed to heal and unify have not lived up to their credo. In fact, they have often done the opposite, setting up barriers between people and commissioning mass murder.

CHAPTER 7

THE ROLE OF RELIGION

One would think that religion would be leading a worldwide effort to promulgate the oneness of humanity. After all, one of the purposes of religion is to inform humanity that we are "children of God" and instruct us about how to behave in his house. It seems only fitting that religion should lead the way in uniting the children of God through the spirit of love and proclaiming the familyhood of man.

Though most people believe in God, humanity is not united and never has been. That does not mean that it was never supposed to be. Some pragmatists might argue that the fact that global unity has not been realized in four million years is a sign that it was never meant to be realized. If we subscribe to that kind of logic, then we would also have to believe that the airplane should never have been invented because it did not already exist. Chances are our world contains many other undiscovered realities that, if discovered, can quicken the pace to achieving true world peace; and religion *should* be leading the way by inspiring and encouraging humanity's quest of the undiscovered realities that are part of our Creator's grand design. We have established that one of those realities is the oneness of humankind.

Religion's Role in Splintering the Human Family

Unfortunately, religion has, by its actions, served primarily to draw us away from that reality. Instead of promulgating the oneness of the human family, traditional organized religion has contributed mightily to the splintering of the human family in the guise of God's work. It has created class systems and hierarchies, thereby establishing a sense of inequality among God's children. This manmade social system, masked in divinity, has been a barrier to humanity's realization of its oneness.

Humanity's own warped interpretations—some well-meaning but naive, and others explicitly self-serving—of the teachings of the Founders of the world's great religions are responsible for this failure. The results of such misinterpretation can be seen in virtually every religion: Many Christians view those who are not baptized as "ruled by Satan"; many Jews feel superior to everyone else because they believe they are the chosen people of God and feel they should avoid interaction with gentiles; many Muslims view those who do not follow the Koran as infidels; a dehumanizing caste system is observed by Hindus. Each religion has had its share of charismatic, illumined interpreters of their Faith's scriptures. These leaders have been the cause of schism and theological competition, which has led to animosity and bloodletting between the various sects and religions throughout the ages.

Internal Religious Quarreling

Internal quarreling within the same religion has been partially responsible for the conflict. According to the *World Christian Encyclopedia* there are at least twenty thousand Christian sects, each with its own slant on Christianity. This has resulted in Christians' killing Christians. Perhaps the most horrendous example of such conflict is World War II, when millions of believers in Jesus killed each other. Christian chaplains prayed for the American and British troops to experience victory and remain unharmed. On the other side, Christian chaplains were praying for German and Italian troops to experience victory and remain unharmed. When the largely Muslim nations of Iran and Iraq clashed in the 1980s, soldiers on both sides prayed to God five times a day while hurling grenades and shooting at each other. Over a million men lost their lives in that war. A Roman Catholic pope in 1935 blessed Italian troops as they went off to conquer Ethiopia, a predominantly Coptic Christian nation ruled by the Christian Emperor Haile Selassie. The bloody conflict between Protestants and Roman Catholics has been going on in Northern Ireland for decades.

The Battling of Major Religions

But internal bickering within religions is not the only reason that religion has been unable to unite the human family. Battling between the major religions has also been a formidable obstacle. For centuries Hindus and Muslims have been at each other's throats in India and elsewhere. From time to time their feuding has erupted into murderous rioting. The Christian crusades directed at wresting control of Palestine (Jesus' birthplace) from the Muslims led to the pillaging of towns and villages, the torture of non-believers, and the death of millions of soldiers and civilians, including women, children, and the elderly. The Roman Catholic Inquisition, established in the 1200s, was designed to eliminate all elements of society who did not conform to the Church's beliefs. Thousands of Jews who refused to convert were hunted down and executed. Those who managed to escape fled their homeland.[1]

Even those Christians who rejected the papacy seemed to share the obsessive hatred of Jews. Martin Luther, who led the Protestant Reformation in what is now Germany, openly reviled Jews as enemies of God, describing them as lecherous creatures, undeserving of acceptance within the human family. At one point he called for all Jews to be condemned to hell.[2]

In their efforts to be faithful, most Christian congregations have embraced the views of their church leaders. In today's era of political correctness, it seems that churchgoers have repressed what they learned about Jews while growing up, but it does not take much for the venom of anti-Semitism to surface and lead to name-calling and pogroms. I believe that Martin Luther's views, as well as the Roman Catholic Church's views, of Jewish people helped to prepare the soil for Nazi anti-Semitic seeds to sprout in Germany and Austria, eventually producing the poisonous fruit of the Holocaust.

There are hate groups today who derive their inspiration from the Christian Bible. They can cite chapter and verse to support their belief that Christianity was meant only for White Protestants. The leadership of the Ku Klux Klan often quotes passages from the Bible in public. Their devotion to their Lord is symbolized by a fiery cross.

There were church-sanctioned hate activities long before the advent of modern Christian-based organizations such as the Ku Klux Klan. In *The Chalice and the Blade,* Riane Eisler cites a number of atrocities executed as a means of preserving the purity of Christianity, not only in Europe, but in Asia and Africa as well. Two in particular stand out:

... in 391 C.E., under Theodosius I, the now thoroughly androcratized

Christians burned the great library in Alexandria [Egypt], one of the last repositories of ancient wisdom and knowledge. And aided and abetted by the man who was later to be canonized Saint Cyril (the Christian bishop of Alexandria), Christian monks barbarously hacked to pieces with oyster shells that remarkable mathematician, astronomer of Alexandria's school of Neoplatonic philosophy, Hypatia. For this woman, now recognized as one of the greatest scholars of all time, was according to Cyril an iniquitous female who had even presumed, against God's commandments, to teach men.[3]

Traditional Attitudes that Divide

The attitudes of traditional religion have also contributed to the disunity of the human family. Where there is no equality there can be no real unity. Women—who represent approximately half of humankind—have been viewed and treated as inferiors by those who have wielded the power. Flawed human interpretations of the teachings of the Divine Educators such as Moses, Jesus Christ, and Muhammad, have found their way into the holy scriptures that are meant to guide and develop the believer's thinking and behavior in society.

For example, in the Bible there are two versions of how humans came into being. In the first chapter of Genesis it states that men and women came into being at the same time, implying equality of the sexes. At the same time, in the second chapter it states that Adam appeared first and, when he became lonely, a woman (Eve) emerged from one of his ribs, implying that man was superior to woman. The early Jewish high priests, the leaders of early Christianity, and Muslim clerics chose the Genesis 2 version of the origin of humanity, hailing it as the truth. I suspect that cultural prejudices toward women must have been a factor in making this choice. And that choice must have influenced the shaping of the Apostle Paul's view of women, which is recorded in the New Testament: "Let a woman learn in silence with all submissiveness. I permit no woman to teach or to have authority over men; she is to keep silent. For Adam was formed first, then Eve; and Adam was not deceived, but the woman was deceived and became a transgressor."[4]

In the 1200s, Thomas Aquinas, whose interpretations of Jesus' teachings helped to frame much of the dogma of the Roman Catholic Church, shared his view of women in his *Summa Theologica:*

> As regards the individual nature, women are defective and misbe-gotten, for the active force in the male seed tends to the production of a perfect likeness in the masculine sex; while the production of women comes from defect in the active force or from some material imposi-tion. . . .[5]

Little has changed in more than seven hundred years. In 1977, Pope Paul VI asserted that women were barred from the priesthood "because our Lord was a man."[6] In the summer of 1998, the Southern Baptist Church, the largest Protestant denomination in the United States, decreed that the husband is the head of the family and that the wife serves God best by serving her husband to the best of her ability.

Most Westerners who have been brought up in a Judeo-Christian society are under the impression that Islam, by design, oppresses women. The media are filled with images of veiled Muslim women who are forbidden to show any part of their body in public, who are viewed as potential temptresses of men. As a consequence they are not allowed to pray with men in their mosques. In some Muslim countries, women who seek an education must attend a segregated all female school that prepares them to be obedient servants to their husbands. In extremist Afghanistan and Iran, women are deprived of many basic human rights, and most men in those lands believe the restrictions imposed upon women to be the will of God.

Such modern-day Muslim practices in relation to gender were not taught by Muhammad, the Founder of Islam. Highly credentialed clerics and philosophers, influenced by cultural biases, have misinterpreted the Prophet's teachings and sayings. Most of Islam's present-day attitudes toward women are based on what Muslims refer to as hadith, which are the narrative record of statements believed to have been made by Muhammed and his companions. Over the centuries, some 600,000 hadith have been collected. Modern Muslim scholars have eliminated 530,000 of them as inauthentic. Of the remaining 7,000, there are two hadith that support the male Muslim rulers' belief in the inherent inferiority of women: "Those who entrust their affairs to a woman will never know prosperity," and "The dog, the ass and woman interrupt prayer if they pass in front of a believer."[7]

What has been done in the name of God by self-proclaimed official spokesmen of God to thwart the realization of a truly united human family is shocking and sad. It has caused tremendous human suffering and delusion, which has been embraced as sacred truth by so many trusting souls. These spokesmen have promulgated the idea that God favors one group of people over another.

The Puritan Church fortified such twisted beliefs. The Puritans were a group of people in England who sincerely wanted to purify their faith. They felt North America would be a place where they could accomplish that mission without opposition from the Anglican Church.

Early Puritan religious leaders reinforced the prevailing theological assumption of inherent human superiority and inferiority. They believed there were groups of people, like themselves, who were chosen to do God's work and that there were also other, more primitive souls, who functioned as agents of Satan.

As a consequence, two leading Puritan theologians, the father-and-son team of Increase and Cotton Mather, supported the slave trade, viewing it as a means of civilizing savages by forcing them to embrace Jesus Christ as their Lord and Savior. These highly respected religious apologists for slavery worked diligently to support their beliefs through biblical evidence. Through careful study, these religious scholars found what they were looking for. They liked to quote the Apostle Paul's call on all servants and slaves to obey their master. One of Increase Mather's sermons directs a warning at the indentured servants in the colony: "You that are servants, have you been guilty of stubborn disobedient carriage toward your masters, though God in His word tells you that you ought to be obedient to them with fear and trembling?"[8]

Both Increase and Cotton Mather found what they considered to be divine evidence that Blacks were destined to occupy a menial level in the social hierarchy. They cited a passage from one of the chapters of Genesis about the curse of Ham, which they took to mean that anyone who was Black was forever branded a lower being. All Puritans, indeed all churchgoers, were exposed to this kind of thinking on a regular basis. The fact that it came from the spokesmen of God in their midst made it easy for them to believe that the enslavement of Black people was God-ordained, sanctioned by the holy scriptures.[9]

This attitude is a factor contributing to the foundation of the social inequality and racial discrimination that has existed in the United States since its inception. For what was taught in church during Colonial times was usually reinforced in the home as well as in school. This form of indoctrination continued when the thirteen colonies became a nation.

The Role of Influential Theologians

The views of great philosophers who considered themselves devout believers in God also played a significant part in bolstering the prevailing view that humanity was composed of superior and inferior groups.

England's John Locke was one of the most influential of these philosophers. Most historians consider him the fashioner of America's political philosophy. This devout Christian, who wrote *The Reasonableness of Christianity* (considered a progressive religious tract in the late1600s), was also considered one of the most liberal political thinkers of the Enlightenment. An Oxford-educated physician and a Crown favorite, Locke believed that human beings are born good, with a clean slate—not as sinners. He thought that an individual's experiences in life would determine his place in society and heaven. Locke railed against the papacy as being too authoritarian and proclaimed that all human beings had the right to life, liberty, and the pursuit of happiness. This great lover of freedom was so revered by Thomas Jefferson that Jefferson wove Locke's ideas about natural rights into the Declaration of Independence. Jefferson also embraced Locke's view of non-Caucasians. Locke believed that democracy was for Whites and slavery for Africans, viewing Black people as subhuman, intended for lifelong service to the White people.[10]

Religion as Champion of the Oppressed and Downtrodden

There are those who will argue that some religions have traditionally championed the cause of the oppressed and downtrodden. While this is true, it does not mean that the leadership and the majority of adherents of those religions truly believed that all people—regardless of skin color, ethnicity, language, culture, and economic development—are equal. Frederick Douglass, the ex-slave who became a forthright champion of social justice in the mid-1800s, saw through his church's façade of brotherhood, proclaiming that American Christianity functioned as a willing agent for slavery and racism:

> The existence of slavery in this country brands . . . your Christianity as a lie. It destroys your moral power abroad; it corrupts your politicians at home. It saps the foundation of religion; it makes your name a hissing and a by-word to a mocking earth. . . .[11]

Some historians cite the work of the Quakers during the era of slavery era in the United States as an example of practicing and promoting the oneness of humankind. It is true that the Quakers officially opposed slavery, and it is true that many Quakers helped to create and maintain the Underground Railroad, which guided runaway slaves to freedom in the North or Canada. Some of the Quaker freedom workers even gave their lives for the human rights cause. Yet, despite the sacrifices these Quakers made, the Quaker Church looked upon those whom they were helping as inferior beings. Blacks and Whites were not allowed to worship side by side. Special benches were set aside for Blacks in Quaker meeting halls. Most parishioners, whether Black or White, understood what the segregated seating meant: Blacks were not quite good enough, or intellectually and socially mature enough, to sit with superior Whites.[12] Though this view was rarely articulated, many Blacks recognized the slight and were moved to establish the Black Christian Church in America. Richard Allen led the way, establishing the African Methodist Episcopal Church in 1818, with Allen serving as its bishop.[13]

Rejection of God's Will

The effort put forth by traditional organized religion to create and preserve a concept that is antithetical to God's will was so thorough, so convincing, that priest and parishioner alike gave little or no credence to the teachings of oneness expounded by the Founders of the world's great religions, who were simply conveying what God had commanded. This grand rejection of God's will has been the cause of untold suffering. It has also left us confused and afraid to explore the possibility that all humans are related to each other.

Based on humanity's behavior over the centuries, it is plain to see that we have not heeded our Creator's appeal to awaken to the reality that every human being belongs to one family. Ample evidence of the appeal is found in the holy scriptures of every great religion:

Judaism: "Have we not all one father? Hath not one God created us?"[14]

". . . Strengthen the bonds of friendship and fellowship among the inhabitants of all lands. Plant virtue in every soul and may the love of Thy name hallow every heart. Praise be Thou, O Lord, our God, giver of peace."[15]

Christianity: "And if a house be divided against itself, that house cannot stand."[16]

"And other sheep I have, which are not of this fold: them also must I bring, and they shall hear my voice; and there shall be one fold, and one shepherd."[17]

Islam: "Hold fast, all together, to God's rope, and be not divided amongst yourselves. . . Let there arise out of you one community, inviting to us all that is good, enjoining what is right, and forbidding what is wrong: those will be prosperous."[18]

"All of God's creatures are His family. He is most beloved of God who does real good to the members of God's family."[19]

Hinduism: " He who experiences the unity of life, sees his own self in all beings, and all beings in his own self, and looks on everything with an impartial eye."[20]

"Whoever sees all beings in himself and in all beings does not, by virtue of such realization, hate anyone. . . When, to that wise sage, all beings are realized as existing in his own self, then what illusion, what sorrow, can afflict him, perceiving as he does the Unity?"[21]

Jainism: "Consider the family of humankind one."[22]

Sikhism: "Do not forget that the world is one great family."[23]

"God is concealed in every heart; His light is in every heart."[24]

Zoroastrian: "Human Nature is good only when it does not do unto another whatever is not good for its own self."[25]

The Bahá'í Faith: ". . . Ye are the fruits of one tree and the leaves of one branch. Deal ye one with another with the utmost love and harmony, with friendliness and fellowship. . . . So powerful is the light of unity that it can illuminate the whole earth."[26]

"The well-being of mankind, its peace and security, are unattainable unless and until its unity is firmly established."[27]

CHAPTER 8

MOVEMENTS TOWARD PEACE

The twentieth century has seen the emergence of a global consciousness of the need to protect human rights. This awakening materialized shortly after World War I and received a boost after World War II. People were tired of war and its devastating effects. There was a collective desire to end hunger, eliminate disease, clean up the planet's atmosphere and waterways. More and more people of influence began to hear a growing cry for social justice.

The victors of World War I heard the call and established the League of Nations in 1920. Sixty-three nations signed on to work at settling geopolitical disputes and reducing armaments in the world. When the League failed, the United Nations (UN) came into being after World War II in 1945 with a resolve to maintain international peace and security. With practically every sovereign nation belonging to the UN, the world organization has expressed confidence that it would not experience the fate of its predecessor.

One of the first acts of the UN was to draft its Universal Declaration of Human Rights, which was revealed to the world in 1948. That charter inspired people of goodwill on all continents to develop nongovernmental organizations (NGOs) that would carry out the letter and spirit of the Declaration of Human Rights. In time, many of them—such as Amnesty International, Oxfam, and the Red Cross—became affiliated with the UN. There are now more than 1,200 NGOs.

While UN agencies and NGOs have made great strides toward eliminating certain diseases, overcoming illiteracy and poverty, settling long-standing intergovernmental disputes, and improving agricultural output in many developing nations, they have done little to correct humanity's fractured view of itself. Although the United Nations Educational, Scientific, and Cultural Organization (UNESCO) drafted and published a paper on the oneness of humankind and it was circulated worldwide, few minds were changed. For the most part, people still cling to the age-old idea that humanity was meant to be segmented into inferior and superior races, ethnicities, and cultures. It did not matter that UNESCO's proclamation was eloquently stated and hailed in many influential quarters as a guide to live by.

It seems that the oneness of humankind remains, for most people, a strange concept that threatens to destabilize their security. Better to adhere to something that is familiar and false than to embrace something unfamiliar but true. It seems that little thought has been given to the devastation and misery this collective mindset has generated.

The Peace Movement

Perhaps the greatest positive result arising from the UN's drive to protect human rights has been the growing universal desire to bring an end to war and establish genuine, lasting peace. Throughout the century a variety of academics, foreign policy experts, enlightened theologians, political philosophers, and human rights activists have been trying to create a scheme that would fulfill the universal desire for peace, but agreement has been hard to come by, even with the advent of the UN. Many independent peace groups came into being, making for a large but uncoordinated peace movement. Despite its large numbers, the movement's lack of coordination has led to constant jockeying for leadership, suspicion of motive, jealousy, rampant backbiting, and cutthroat competition for members among the various groups, leading ultimately to the demise of the movement. Undoubtedly, the end of the Cold War has also had something to do with the failure of the movement. With Russia and the United States no longer being enemies, the prospects of world peace were greater than ever before in modern history. As a result, more and more peace activists channeled their energies into solving other social problems such as pollution, crime, and drug abuse.

From the 1920s to the late 1980s, many people in both the East and the West felt that Marxism held the greatest promise for achieving global peace and uniting the human family. The Bolshevik Revolution in Russia was viewed by many among the world's intelligentsia as the dawn of a new era for which all people of goodwill had been longing. Embracing Marxist-Leninist thought, they envisioned a world in which poverty would no longer exist, where everyone would have a job and enough to eat, where there would no longer be any worry about paying medical bills, where classism, racism, and sexism would be eliminated. The vision of such a socialist society held strong appeal for many academics and for many developing nations around the world. Impressed by the tremendous economic and social progress the Soviet Union and the People's Republic of China were able to make within a very short time, developing nation after developing nation adopted socialism. When Soviet Premier Nikita Khruschev predicted at a UN General Assembly session in 1962 that socialism would eventually bury capitalism, the majority of delegates from the nations represented in that chamber probably believed the prediction to be true.

When the Soviet Union eventually began to unravel in the late 1980s, most of the other socialist governments collapsed as well. No longer distracted by an incessant outpouring of boastful propaganda, the rest of the world began to get a closer look at the actual workings of the socialist states. It became apparent that, while their constitutions outlawed racism, classism, and sexism, these forms of discrimination continued to exist unabated. While everyone who was willing to work had a job, there were shortages of food and living space, medical care was poor, pollution abounded, and, in time, the fear of sharing one's true thoughts and feelings in public or in private deadened the spirit of the people. What had appeared at first to be unity had proved itself to be little more than an enforced, dull, gray, uniformity that bred a sense of weariness.

While socialism has failed, and former socialist states are experimenting with capitalism during the post-Cold War period, the longing for genuine world peace remains. This longing has only intensified as ancient ethnic rivalries have erupted into bloody clashes and as terrorism has reared its ugly head more and more frequently in both East and West.

Sadly, the efforts to find a pathway to peace have not included recognizing and practicing the principle of the oneness of humankind. Those who had the power to institute change and pave the way for a new, enlightened course of action had reasons to shun this reality. There was a general fear of the unknown and a deep-rooted resistance to change. There were also those who would not accept the reality of the oneness of humankind because they were convinced that man is merely an animal, albeit it the smartest animal alive, struggling to survive in the jungle of life. Those who held positions of political or religious leadership feared that taking a new course would result in a loss of power and would upset the stability of their communities. Leaders of industry felt the same way. For some of these leaders, rejecting the reality of the oneness of humankind was a painful decision because they secretly believed in it. What would inspire them to reveal their secret? A universally respected figure openly advocating and vigorously campaigning for everyone to embrace the reality of oneness.

The twentieth century has witnessed a number of extraordinary leaders who have expressed their belief in the oneness of humankind and their hope that one day all humanity will embrace the same vision. People such as Albert Einstein, Mahatma Gandhi, Helen Keller, Dr. Martin Luther King, Jr., Eleanor Roosevelt, and Albert Schweitzer dared to make known their belief in the oneness of humankind and their hope that humanity will someday be united.

To the visionary Pierre Teilhard De Chardin, the principle of the oneness of humankind was obvious: "We are one, after all, you and I; together we suffer, together exist, and forever will recreate ourselves."[1] Eric Erikson, a noted psychologist and philosopher who shared the same vision, appealed to his fellowman to open his eyes and see what is so apparent: "The question is: Will mankind realize that it is one species—or is it destined to remain divided into 'pseudo-species' forever playing out one (necessarily incomplete) version of mankind against all others?"[2]

The vision was shared under dramatic and memorable circumstances in 1963 on the steps of the Lincoln Memorial in Washington, D.C., when Martin Luther King, Jr., through television and communication satellite, revealed his dream of a world in which the human family is united and people will be judged not by the color of their skin but by the content of their character.

Unfortunately, humanity remains fragmented. Those who took to heart what seers like King and Gandhi shared in terms of the oneness of humankind seek each other out. Small in number, they gather from time to time at World Federalist and United Nations Association meetings where they try to rekindle their enthusiasm for spreading the truth about oneness.

But their voice is not even a whisper in the hurly-burly, dog-eat-dog atmosphere that dominates our communities. Nevertheless, the pursuit for peace is still alive. But not always for humane reasons. I have observed that some folks promote peace because of their fear of death or of the annihilation of their comfortable lifestyle. Seeking an end to human suffering and establishing social justice appear to be secondary interests.

The Multicultural Movement

Determined to end war and terrorism and the persecution of minorities, a non-controversial movement promoting tolerance has taken hold in North America, much of Europe, and countries such as Australia, Singapore, and Japan. The aim of this movement is to get everyone to become tolerant of one another, regardless of background and allegiances. International organizations such as the UN and various national and local governments and influential foundations have endorsed this effort, which has gained considerable popular support. A great deal of money is being poured into projects that call for appreciating and respecting the differences between people of different cultures, ethnic groups, and religions.

The celebration of diversity has spread widely. Schools almost everywhere promote it, as do churches, synagogues, corporations, labor unions, fraternal organizations, and foundations. Many who are committed to the cause of multiculturalism believe they have found a way to peace that most people can support. Not surprisingly, those who promote this movement with the greatest ardor are middle-class Whites and certain groups that have a vested interest in ensuring that they are respected without interference in the way they operate. Preservation of existing cultures, as they are presently constituted, has become the battle cry of the ardent multiculturalists. They want to believe that their culture functions today the way it did when it first came into being, but believing that is to reject the basic flow of nature.

Why? Because culture, which is the way of life of a particular group of people, is not a static phenomenon. While culture is always in the process of changing, the pace of change can differ widely. In the past, change has generally occurred more rapidly in cities than in rural areas.[3] Today, however, because of the influence of the media and the advent of the personal computer, cultural changes taking place in the city influence those in the hinterland much faster than ever before in the history of humankind.

Persistent and aggressive resistance to change breeds suspicion and fear within a culture. Any outside influence is viewed as a threat, setting off a collective urge to strike out at any potential carrier of "different" ways or ideas.

Ideally, different ideas and ways of doing things should be welcomed. They do not have to be adopted, but it should be recognized that they may offer alternatives that could improve the quality of life within a culture and broaden its outlook. The British culture is a case in point. The cold, stiff-upper-lip image of the British has changed with the influx of Africans, West Indians, Pakistanis, and Indians after World War II. Their cultures have blended with that of the British, making for a more vibrant, dynamic, and liberated people producing music, art, dance, and technologies that would have put Queen Victoria in a permanent state of shock. The benefits have been tangible: According to the influential British news weekly *The Economist,* the streams of immigrants from various parts of the British Commonwealth who made Britain their home provided a mighty boost to the nation's sagging economy.[3] They came with an enthusiasm for the freedoms Britain offered and with a desire to do as well as possible in every way.

Certainly we all benefit from learning about different cultures, for it helps to broaden our outlook. But when only the differences are stressed, as they are in most multicultural programs, lingering suspicions about ethnic mixing and intermarriage are reinforced. This kind of emphasis can lead impressionable minds to believe that the Chinese, Swedes, Nigerians, Lakotas, Cubans, Malays, and other groups are different species.

This impression is not merely the result of sloppy program design. There are reasons to believe that some influential proponents of multiculturalism purposely stress cultural differences in their slick, heavily financed programs as a means of preventing the extinction of their own culture and preserving its "purity" and social advantage. Institutions that pay for multicultural programs are often so desperate to find ways to avoid racial eruption in their schools or places of work that they do not take time to assess the real slant of the programs.

The advocates of cultural "purity," operating within the purview of multiculturalism, seem to be achieving their goal of institutionalizing cultural separatism. This is skillfully done by billboarding terms such as "toleration" and "respect" in their literature and public announcements. These are the terms most people associate with goodness, human rights, justice, and equality—terms that most people of goodwill find attractive and comfortable. Taking advantage of the prevailing fears associated with interracial encounters and of the desire for social tranquillity, these sophisticated purveyors of cultural separatism have defined toleration and respect as a condition in which every culture does its own thing without any positive or negative interference from outsiders. To uphold their image as human-rights advocates, they may engage in charity work for the economically disadvantaged of other ethnic groups, perhaps participating in an intercultural festival once or twice a year, but regular intercultural fraternizing is avoided as much as possible. On almost every university campus, in every school in a so-called integrated neighborhood, Black and White students avoid interaction with each other. This is most evident in the schools' dining halls and cafeterias, on the school grounds, and in nearby shops and restaurants. There, one can observe a sophisticated form of apartheid in America that most people are willing to tolerate if it is what is needed to ensure community safety and peace.

It is not surprising that some multicultural programs never urge people of different ethnic groups to love each other. The word "love" is missing from their texts because love can lead to unity, the serious mixing and banding together of ethnic groups, and this could lead to the materialization of their unstated fear of intermarriage. By the same token, one rarely sees the word "unity" in materials promoting multiculturalism. What is vigorously emphasized instead—often through dazzling presentations—is an appreciation for each ethnic group's uniqueness. Perhaps the greatest evidence of the success of the multiculturalist movement is that love and unity are not mentioned as goals in leading conferences, speeches, and literature on race relations. Leading race relations pundits avoid such terms because tolerance, not unity, is their aim. But tolerance is a fragile condition, which only curtails prejudicial behavior and does not eradicate the prejudice, for a rumor or an irrational remark can reactivate it.

Another concern is that encouraging mere cultural toleration can contribute to condoning human rights violations and perpetuating social injustice. Some cultures, for example, support a strict caste system. In India, according to custom, an untouchable is not allowed to step in the shadow of a Brahmin. To do so could result in the untouchable's death while authorities look the other way. And there are other tolerated violations of human rights. For example, a cultural custom that calls for young women who reach puberty to undergo a physically painful and psychologically damaging circumcision rite, unjustified by any medical reasoning. Equally distasteful is the "chosen people" status that some cultures claim as their own. All humans are God's children.

Championing diversity has encouraged people to become more "politically correct," created a fragile atmosphere of peaceful coexistence and polite aloofness. It has failed to overcome the feelings of superiority and inferiority, suspicion and anger, fear and hostility that members of different cultures harbor toward each other. Though a sincere effort is made to conceal such negative feelings, they remain nonetheless festering in the subconscious until a rumor or irrational remark brings them to the surface. Under such conditions no true and abiding peace can be established. At best, a brittle truce is arranged, its longevity dependent on pretense and conflict avoidance.

To truly appreciate diversity, we must internalize the principle of the oneness of humankind. This enables us to truly understand that the person who looks different from us is nevertheless a member of the same family. We find we have a natural impulse to respect that person—a genuine desire to care for him, work with him, and appreciate the unique talents he can offer toward improving the quality of life in our community. Instead of viewing him with suspicion and fear, we trust him because we see him as a brother. Like branches of the same tree, each branch has a particular function in helping the tree to fulfill its purpose.

To try to appreciate diversity without understanding the oneness of humankind is like expecting a rootless tree to remain standing. No amount of propping can keep it upright. The same is true of multiculturalism. Its aims are too narrow, too shallow to be an effective catalyst for peace, for it subtly opposes heartfelt intercommunity cohesion and promotes separatism. By doing so, it keeps us from exploring the reality of the oneness of humankind, which is the first step toward establishing true peace.

After all is said and done, all of the activities and expenditures of great sums of money to promote diversity produces little advancement in unifying the human family.

Where to Go from Here

If humanity is to realize true peace once and for all, all members of the human family must work to remove their blinders, overcome their prejudices, set aside their animosities, and summon the courage to commit themselves to creating unity. As mentioned earlier, the establishment of unity hinges on the wholehearted acceptance of oneness. Rejecting the reality of oneness without open-mindedly investigating it is like closing one's eyes and swearing that there is no sun. When oneness is internalized, a person develops an irresistible urge to bring people together, especially those who have traditionally distrusted one another. Such a person becomes a force for unity in his or her community. Imagine what would happen in a community if most of its inhabitants were to develop that urge.

Philosopher Martin Buber, a Jewish existentialist, implored his fellow human beings to embrace their familyhood, believing that their failure to do so could lead to their demise: "In the closed sphere of the exclusively political, there is no way to penetrate to the factual of men nor to relieve the existential mistrust which divides the world into hostile camps . . . whose 'natural end' is the technically perfect suicide of the human race." Therefore, "The solidarity of all separate groups in the flaming battle for the becoming of one humanity is," he believed, "in the present hour, the highest duty on earth. . . . ."[4]

CHAPTER 9

AN EMERGING PATTERN OF PROGRESS

Today's unprecedented defense of human rights and incessant groping for peace are not merely acts of desperation; they are positive steps leading toward the widespread realization that all human beings are related. This movement toward recognizing the oneness of humanity, though noticed by few, continues regardless. Humanity moves toward its unification, just as clans in the past were drawn together to form tribes. Necessity, more than anything else, has always been the driving force. There seems to be a pattern to this grand social evolution: When the time is right, humanity advances toward the fulfillment of its destiny, the oneness of humankind.

The Trend toward International Collective Security

This process is dependent on certain events to quicken its pace. Though the events may, at the time, seem meaningless to even the most learned of people, their significance is easily understood in retrospect. For example, the movement toward unity received a significant push forward in the mid-1930s when the League of Nations ordered sanctions against Italy for invading Ethiopia. International sanctions toward a rogue nation had never been leveled before. Though few nations upheld the sanctions, an important international precedent was set. Some fifty years later, when the United Nations ordered that sanctions be leveled against Iraq for invading Kuwait, the sanctions were upheld. For the first time in the history of humankind, a truly international collective security effort was launched, setting another precedent, and Iraq was forced out of Kuwait. A few years later, many nations were inspired to organize and carry out a military effort to bring about peace in war-ravaged Bosnia-Herzegovina. It appears that a trend has emerged. Looking to the future, one can reasonably expect that in time, international intervention to maintain world peace, curb terrorist activity, and overcome major violations of human rights will become commonplace. An international police force, staffed and funded by every nation in the world, will evolve. It will not only put down any attempts by tyrants to annex lands that do not belong to them, it will also come to the rescue of people ravaged by earthquakes, hurricanes, and other natural disasters. These changes will be realized despite the fact that the great majority of humanity is unaware of what is really happening, and despite stiff opposition from forces fearful of change.

Two Steps Forward, One Step Backward

It appears that we are in the midst of another surge forward in the unification process. Advances in communications and transportation technology, as well as the swelling of the Earth's population, are drawing together people who have never interacted before. People of diverse ethnicities are living next to each other and working side by side.

Though the unprecedented integration of ethnic neighborhoods that were once strictly segregated is occurring in many places, the sudden interfacing of different cultures is fraught with danger, for people who have never had anything to do with one another before are usually suspicious of one another. Fear, a by-product of ignorance, permeates both sides. Open-mindedness evaporates, and in many instances alienation and friction result.

But such occurrences should not be viewed as proof that the unity of humankind is a pipe dream. Differences, as well as initial suspicion and fear, are to be expected. Whenever human social evolution has experienced a surge forward, most people have been unable to understand or accept the changes immediately. The normal human tendency in such situations has been to avoid acknowledging what was happening. Considerable energy has often gone into denying the changes, but it never negates them. For example, tribes that had been fighting each other for centuries, vowing never to come together, eventually united to form nations. Again, the mergers arose from necessity when the tribes simply got tired of fighting each other. Through trial and error, and perhaps in some cases divine intervention, a new set of values emerged and was embraced, and the tribes decided to unite. A more current example can be seen in the formation and development of the European Union, which has turned ancient, bitter foes who have fought in two horrific world wars into allies who now use the same currency and passports. All of these changes constitute steps toward the eventual unification of the human family. It has been a two-steps-forward one-step-backward type of advancement. Following the tendency to focus on what is wrong, the step backward usually receives the most attention, fueling the skeptics' and cynics' argument that humanity is unable to unite. Nevertheless, the movement toward embracing oneness—the essential stepping-stone to unity—forges ahead.

The fact that modern science recognizes that all human beings are biologically related will in time overcome whatever barriers prevent the majority of people from embracing the reality of the oneness of humankind. It takes time for what science uncovers to penetrate the consciousness of the generality of humankind—at least that has been the case in the past. The greatest barrier has always been, and continues to be, our emotional attachment to falsehoods we assume to be the truth. But perhaps the accelerating pace of change will shorten the length of time it will take for people to overcome their prejudices and wholeheartedly embrace the principle of the oneness of humankind. Certainly, when our schools begin incorporating in their curricula the findings of modern science regarding the oneness of humankind, the barriers will come down faster than many people anticipate.

A Growing Desire for Truth

Because the reality of the oneness of the human family has always existed despite humanity's inability to understand or to practice it, some seekers of truth are asking why this principle should receive such heavy emphasis now in particular. The reason is that humanity has reached the threshold of its maturity. During the stages of its infancy, childhood, and adolescence, humanity did not have the sense, and certainly not the wisdom, to recognize its essential oneness. Misguided religious and political leaders, believing that they were the wisest of all, led their followers astray, inculcating distorted views of the structure of humanity. As a consequence, men and women went about their lives believing that there were superior and inferior groups of people, smarter and less intelligent groups of people. They believed intercultural marriage to be sinful and accepted all sorts of other unfounded theories that were propounded as the truth by leading thinkers of the day, giving credence to prevailing fractured views of the structure of humanity. Whatever the most respected theologians and philosophers believed and taught was usually embraced without question by others. Today, more people than ever before are obtaining an education, rendering them less dependent on others in decision making, seeking the truth, and developing their own beliefs. It seems that there is around the world a growing desire to engage in an unfettered search for truth.

Though it may appear that those who sincerely question the authenticity of existing institutions and seek the truth are in the minority, more and more people are beginning to question the validity and usefulness of practices and traditions they have never questioned before. In time, the introspective questioning will be shared with others, eventually producing a critical mass of people who are willing to embrace change.

The Accelerating Pace of Change

Some attribute this growing awakening to the spirit of a new age, yet they have no idea of its source, nor do they express any interest in knowing what is the origin of this spiritual infusion that seems to be shaking the very foundations of the existing social order. All they know is that they cannot look to the past for guidance anymore, for they feel that the tired and ineffectual institutions of today were fashioned in the past and are unable to cope adequately with the unprecedented complex issues of this day. Their view of the future is blurred. New and fresh ways of doing things are needed. As a result, considerable experimentation is occurring at many different levels, producing amazing discoveries and new trends. The rate of discovery has been mind-boggling, bringing about changes in living patterns and outlooks. Old and well-established ideas are being replaced by new ones, causing a reconfiguration of how we view the world. It has also set off a collective set of mixed emotions. Hope as well as uncertainty dominate most people's thinking. Not knowing what to expect normally generates such feelings. After all, we are witnessing the development of new movements and institutions, all necessary innovations in the surge toward the unification of the human family.

A burgeoning global economy has emerged in which national tariffs are disappearing. More corporations are adopting flexible work schedules, instituting profit sharing, establishing physical fitness centers for employees, and giving the average worker a voice in the way the firm is managed. More and more corporations located in different countries are merging. Products assembled in one nation are often made from parts manufactured in many other countries. All of these developments would have been absolutely foreign and unacceptable to the men who drove the engines of the industrial revolution.

More schools are instituting an interdisciplinary approach to education. There is a growing use of modern technologies such as computers and television in schools. More and more students are being exposed to peace and ecology programs and getting involved in community service projects. The number of people attending college is growing. Some schools are promoting world citizenship. An appreciation for diversity is being stressed.

Institutional health care is being provided to more people then ever before. Diseases such as smallpox, polio, tuberculosis, measles, whooping cough, and mumps have been practically eliminated through international vaccine programs. Organ and gene transplants are saving lives. New surgical techniques have been developed to shorten operation procedures and hasten recovery. New disease-healing drugs are being developed almost every day. Scientists have learned more about the human brain in the past five years than in the previous one hundred; this explosion of new knowledge has led scientists to a greater understanding of the brain's biology.[1] By stressing a holistic approach to health care, people in many nations are becoming more nutrition and exercise conscious and are thus living longer.

Through an explosion of inventions in the twentieth century, people are traveling more, learning more, being exposed to different cultures and becoming more globally conscious. In transportation, automobiles are capable of going 120 miles per hour, trains at 200 miles per hour, commercial planes at 700 miles per hour. Rockets are able to hurl space stations into orbit above the Earth. Through the wonders of television and communications satellites, people in Morocco are able to learn about the people of Ecuador and their ways, and vice versa.

One hundred years ago, no cellular phones, transistor radios, digital televisions, robotics, computerized harvesters, communications satellites, or fiber optics existed; nor did the Internet or any of its amazing services. Today, one has only to push a set of computer keys to engage in a conversation with persons in Calcutta, Brasilia, Nairobi, and Nome in a matter of seconds. If people living a hundred years ago were to live today, they would be astounded by the social changes the twentieth century has witnessed: Women are now heading corporations, soaring around our planet as astronauts, conducting symphony orchestras, and competing with men as horse-racing jockeys. There are no more empires. The traditionally disenfranchised are gaining access to privileges once reserved only for the elite; they are attending schools, breaking into the professional ranks, exercising the right to vote, and serving on juries. Children of former headhunters are now graduating from universities. The number of interracial families is growing. More and more legal systems are recognizing hate crimes as violations of the law.

The social and industrial changes have been accompanied by equally significant geopolitical changes: Colonialism is dead; absolute monarchy has all but died out; nations are now pooling their resources in common market arrangements; ancient colonial enemies are now allies. The European Union, for example, has become a trendsetter for other nations on different continents which are now following suit. International collective security systems are now dealing with acts of geopolitical tyranny. Long-standing traditions and lifestyles have been replaced by an outpouring of liberal expression reflected in a new age of art, music, and dance. Issues once considered taboo are being openly debated in public; once-private activities are being practiced openly. Journalism has become far more wide-ranging and penetrating in its coverage. Sweatshops have been discovered and exposed, as have systems of forced child labor. People who never knew freedom are now free.

Progressive change is occurring so swiftly that most people have given little thought to what is causing all of it, for they are preoccupied with making timely adjustments and weighing which of the changes should be integrated into their lifestyles. Making the right decisions is not easy, for many of the changes are viewed as an assault on long-honored traditions and deeply rooted values. Perplexed, some people see the changes as fads, working hard to convince themselves that the changes will soon revert or fade away. But many are taking root, causing deep apprehension among people who focus on the negative results and trust only the status quo. Concentrating on the one step backward, these people are blind to the two steps taken forward toward the unification of humanity. History has shown that progressive changes usually encounter strong opposition, especially since the changes initially are not fully understood by those who adopt them; as a result, some frightening social practices develop that scare others.

While many new freedoms have emerged, the institution of marriage is weakening, and the rate of divorce is soaring. There are more single-parent families today than ever before. Giving birth to children outside of wedlock has become a common occurrence; sexual activity is increasing among pre-teen-agers; AIDS has become a global plague. In dealing with the new freedoms, humanity is acting like a child who is forbidden to eat candy, finding himself alone in a candy shop with a lot of money. In many ways, people are gorging themselves on their newly found freedom, causing major disruptions of established ways. Traditionalists see anarchy replacing government by law. Age-old norms that have assured community tranquillity for centuries are giving way to a laissez-faire attitude that resists any form of control. Media censorship is practically nonexistent. A new morality that borders on amorality is emerging. An "anything goes" attitude is gaining momentum, especially among youth and young adults, and more and more middle-aged and elderly folks, seeking an elixir that will slow the aging process, are turning to the ways that have captured the young ones' hearts. Ethics seem to have been redefined to reflect the libertine spirit of the new age. Sex has become more of a service than an expression of love. Hedonism abounds. The worship of "things" is growing, while faith in conventional religion is fading.

In many quarters, the freewheeling spirit of the sixties and seventies, which resulted in large-scale repudiation of many time-honored traditions, still lives, and this scares many people. Some are so fearful that they seek refuge in religious fundamentalism, believing that they will be protected from what they feel is perversion resulting from unrestrained freedom. The emergence of this reactionary force is dividing communities and exacerbating existing prejudices. As fear has risen, many people have developed a "bunker" mentality. Others find limited solace in a wide assortment of escape routes. Drugs and alcohol are leading the way, causing serious social problems. Drunken driving fatalities are rising, as are spousal abuse and child abuse.

Changes are occurring so swiftly that many people are hesitant to watch the news on television or read the newspaper. They sense chaos and long for the "good old days," not realizing that they were good only for a select few that did not include the ancestors of most of those who clamor for a return to the past.

The Twin Processes of Growth and Decline

Fortunately, some people are able to see order in the chaos. They see clearly the two-steps-forward and one-step-backward process. They are able to discern two forces at work in the world, both operating simultaneously: One is growth, or the process of unification; the other is decline, or the process of disintegration. With each passing day the pace of growth and decline, unification and disintegration quickens. As a result, the world is getting both better and worse at the same time. On the one hand, the process of decline and disintegration continues unabated until it expires; on the other hand, the process of growth and unification continues, becoming more recognizable and influential and gaining momentum. These twin processes are part of a grand transformation in which all that is obsolete fades away and is replaced by what the growth force produces. One can argue that the force of decline is progressive, because whatever is outdated, reactionary, or oppressive will eventually decline or disintegrate, making way for services and institutions that will help human beings prosper in a united world. In effect, the world to which we have become accustomed is being rolled up, and a new one is replacing it.

Sadly, most people are unaware of the twin processes of growth and decline. Blinded by fear, apathy, suspicion, and hopelessness, they see only the decline and its ravages. Life, to them, is a sinking ship; they spend considerable time searching for rafts.

Those who are aware of the twin processes are hopeful and optimistic, for they have a sense of what the unification process will lead to. For them, this day is a time of great promise. Their positive outlook is not the result of wishful thinking, delusion, or a Pollyannish attitude; nor is it the result of strict adherence to some philosopher's outlandish theory. What is happening, they feel, is an evolutionary thrust—something that is meant to be—as unstoppable as the passage from childhood to adulthood. The extreme reactions to the changes, both positive and negative, will pass. It is only natural for those who have been deprived of certain rights and freedoms to express themselves in an exaggerated fashion. In time, their passion will moderate, and the reasons for the opposition to the changes will be understood. Progress is rarely accepted without challenge, and in most instances the challenge is vigorous. It is only natural for the old to resist the new, for the unknown to be viewed with suspicion. Though opposition usually leads to friction, in the long run it usually has the effect of forcing those who introduce the changes to refine and improve them. Battered and bruised, we forge ahead in the God-sent push toward unification.

Philosopher Alfred North Whitehead cautioned that meaningful progress does not come easily in this world: "The major advances in civilization are processes which all but wreck the societies in which they occur."[2] Progress and hardship seem to go hand in hand. The process of human birth demonstrates this principle: Much pain is experienced before the fruit of the labor is produced.

Some of the most respected thinkers of our time are aware of the twin processes operating in the world today. Václav Havel, President of the Czech Republic, is one such leader. In a speech delivered in Philadelphia in July 1994, he shared the following:

There are good reasons for suggesting that the modern age has ended. Many things indicate that we are going through a transitional period, when it seems that something is on the way out and something else is painfully being born. It is as if something were crumbling, decaying and exhausting itself, while something else, still indistinct, was arising from the rubble.[3]

President Havel realizes that we live in a new age, an age of transition from an old world order to a new one. Every day brings fresh evidence of the collapse of old ideas and institutions and the blossoming of new ones.

Pierre Teilhard de Chardin, one of the great visionaries of the twentieth century, was also aware of the direction in which humanity is headed:

I can see only one way of escape from this state of uncertainty which threatens to paralyze all positive action: we must rise above the storm, the chaos of surface detail, and from a higher vantage-point look for the outline of some great and significant phenomenon. To rise up so as to see clearly is what I have tried to do, and it has led me to accept, however improbable they may appear, the reality and the consequences of the major cosmic process which, for want of a better name, I have called "human planetization."[4]

For optimists, this is an exciting time in which to live; for others it is a frightening time. The optimist awakens each morning wondering what wonderful thing is going to happen today; his counterpart awakens wondering what awful things are going to occur. What they have in common is their unawareness of what is causing the monumental changes. Sadly, if they were to be told, they would probably reject the finding. Their emotional attachment to falsehoods they believe to be truths would most likely prevent them from recognizing and embracing what they seek.

History has a way of repeating itself. According to historian Arnold Toynbee, spiritually inspired civilizations come into being from time to time. In the beginning, they infuse a spirit of hope into the community. The moral consciousness of the people is deepened. New ideas replace old. There is elasticity of thinking, which produces inventions that help to make living easier. Community unity is strengthened, and human evolution advances, drawing us closer to the day when the human family is unified.

But in time, Toynbee points out, the flexibility and openness that helped to make the civilization benevolently productive are replaced by rigidity and narrow-mindedness. The spirit of hope that once inspired people is replaced by suspicion. Man-made dogmas prevent people from seeing the Divine light. The community becomes fragmented, pessimism and cynicism abound, and a sense of hopelessness weighs heavily on people's hearts.

Yet, while one civilization is crumbling, Toynbee explains, another is always emerging, viewed at first as an obscure minority. He cites the early Christians as an example of such an emerging civilization. The Roman leadership considered the Christians to be nothing more than a small, insignificant Jewish sect and predicted its early demise. These learned men proved to be poor prognosticators.

Impressed with the love the early Christians showed toward others and by their willingness to sacrifice themselves for the benefit of others, the Roman emperor Constantine embraced the new religion, believing it alone would preserve the empire.[5]

If Toynbee's interpretation of history is correct, then there must be a minority in the world today who possesses the germinating seeds of a global civilization, all of whose inhabitants view themselves as family members.

CHAPTER 10

THE COMING OF AGE
OF HUMANITY

When we internalize the reality of the oneness of humankind, we become able to see possibilities we would never have seen in our previous state of mind. Our view of reality broadens and deepens. We are enabled to see realities we never saw before. The idea of the Earth's being one country no longer seems like a pipe dream. In fact, we begin to view the internationalization of our planet as a necessary step toward establishing world peace, and we find we want to dedicate ourselves to sharing with others what we now feel is so obvious. When a great number of people attain such an outlook, individuals and institutions will undergo metamorphosis. As a result, the collective spirit in the world will be more caring and optimistic than it is today. Changes that once seemed impossible before we embraced the concept of oneness will begin to seem realistic, workable, and manageable.

Dismantling False Beliefs

What will the world look like when most of us have internalized the fact that we are all related? Before answering that question, another question needs to be addressed: What must we do to recognize and internalize that reality? To answer that question, we need to understand the kind of mindset that develops when one is attached to the long-standing fractured view of the structure of humanity. This understanding will help us to avoid repeating the mistakes that have contributed to the entrenchment of false beliefs and will put us in a better position to dismantle them. Just as a demolition engineer needs to know how a building is constructed before he can effectively demolish it without polluting the atmosphere and without hurting anyone, we need to understand the mindset we hope to dismantle before we can effectively combat it.

Our Present-Day Emotional and Spiritual State

Because people have for so long harbored a fractured view of the structure of humanity, that view has become ingrained in their consciousness as a reality, a principle—as if it were an eternal verity. Through the years, there have been no large-scale protestations clamoring for a change of view. To have done so would have been tantamount to questioning the existence of a reality as universally accepted as gravity. The fractured view of the structure of humanity has remained fixed in people's minds and rooted in their hearts. As a consequence, a pattern of separate social, political, and religious entities has emerged. This pattern of separation has become as natural to us as the sun, the moon, and the air we breathe.

This deeply rooted separation has led to the formation of an us-versus-them mentality that is reflected in virtually every phase of life—in human relationships as well as in the geopolitical realm. It often turns patriotism into a fanatical chauvinism and pride that breed disdain for other people and other nations. Being "number one" and maintaining that position is seen as the pinnacle of attainment, while preferring others over oneself is viewed as foolish and impractical, if not crazy, notwithstanding our admiration for the altruism of extraordinary individuals such as Harriet Tubman or Mother Teresa.

Fulfilling one's personal interests and obtaining personal satisfaction are valued above cooperation, and the urge to beat the competition often becomes a raging goal. Such attitudes give rise to selfishness, suspicion, distrust, fear, anxiety, greed, and the impulse to do battle with anyone who seriously disagrees with us or threatens the accomplishment of our goals. The battling can be physical or mental and can lead to long-lasting feuds and grudges, which widen the chasm of misunderstanding between individuals, groups, and even nations. Such conditions create uncertainty and insecurity, which, when prolonged, can result in a fatalistic pessimism that sometimes degenerates into hopelessness. Paranoia and suspicion abound, creating an adversarial atmosphere in which negotiation, even discussion, usually pits two attacking parties against each other in an attempt to find and exploit one another's weaknesses. Winning, rather than gaining understanding, is emphasized. The end-justifies-the-means approach becomes the popular means of accomplishment, leading to the development of a dog-eat-dog outlook in the community. Friction and tension, rather than harmony, tend to dominate daily life, and daily living becomes a struggle. When the desire for change becomes strong, yet no acceptable course of action seems available to achieve it, some people will strike out blindly and violently. Others will develop a bunker mentality, spending most of their time looking for ways to dull the pain.

Ironically, while they desperately search for an escape, the innate eternal spark of hope remains alive within them. Deep in their subconscious there is a feeling that somehow things will get better, and this feeling keeps most people plodding onward; otherwise there would be far more suicides than there are. Even cynics possess this spark of hope, though it is buried more deeply in the subconscious, for most cynics are disillusioned idealists who have wholeheartedly embraced a cause that has proven fraudulent or grown corrupt and thus failed to achieve its goals.

Racism, classism, sexism, and the growing disparity between the rich and the poor—problems that have plagued humanity for centuries, causing incalculable suffering and rage—are due to humanity's distorted view of itself. Rich and poor, Black and White, Arab and Jew, as well as hundreds of other ethnic groups live in separate worlds, harboring twisted impressions of each other that reinforce their suspicions toward people who seem different. The invisible barriers that keep people apart become a means of ensuring security. Considerable energy is expended to fortify the barriers, the rationale being that avoidance prevents conflict, and where there is no conflict there will be no violence. Survival becomes the dominant goal. In a sense, our world functions as a prison, locking various ethnic groups, cultures, and religions into separate cells.

What has just been described is, for the most part, a general portrait of humanity's present-day emotional and spiritual state, but it is not how we were meant to be. When the majority of humanity finally recognizes and internalizes the oneness of humankind, a different worldwide emotional state will exist—the state, I believe, that our Creator has in mind for us and expects us to attain. To ensure that we attain it, He has endowed us with the capacity to become a force for unity in our lifetime. When we recognize and develop that capacity, we acquire an entirely different outlook than most people manifest today. That capacity exists in the latent divine qualities of every soul. The more these qualities are developed, the more attractive we become to others, and the more attractive others become to us. We see only the good in whomever we meet. No one is a stranger; everyone is a family member, and the desire to love and protect our family members is fulfilled with a sense of joy. In this condition we possess a powerful urge to draw people together in a spirit of love and gently familiarize them with their familial ties.

To those who have already internalized the principle of the oneness of humanity, the scenario I am about to describe will not seem strange or unattainable. In fact, it will seem perfectly logical, absolutely real, and meant to be. However, those who are unaware of the principle, or those who have given it little thought, may find what I am about to share outrageous, perhaps even arrogant.

Believe me, I am no one special. I do not possess extraordinary metaphysical powers. I am not a professional seer. Far from it! The description that follows is based solely on my understanding of the thinking, attitudes, and behaviors that are manifested by people who have internalized and begun to practice the principle of the oneness of humankind—people who know themselves, understand their spiritual nature, and recognize the purpose of life. Those who are governed by a "me first" philosophy, or who look to the past for hope and guidance, will most likely view my attempt to describe the future as sheer fantasy or may see it as a threat. In the end, it is a matter of choice. Do we want to continue to follow the path of decline and disunity or tread the path of growth and unity? If we choose the latter, I feel we will find ourselves living in a world something like the scenario that follows.

The World of the Future

Human understanding will have evolved to the point where we will all see our planet as our common home, where no tariffs exist; no visas or passports are required; a common language is spoken; a common system of morals is practiced; differences in personality, temperament, taste, aesthetics, vocation, and belief are appreciated; hunger does not exist; education is provided for all; genuine care and affection are afforded the elderly; children feel secure; the sick are comforted; displays of egotism are rare; and service-centered consultation is employed to administer the affairs of the household. As in every healthy home, all of the Earth's occupants, regardless of skin color, ethnicity, gender, and religion are considered family and are united. Love, not hatred, is the dominating spirit in the home. The family members openly show their love for one another and find pleasure in serving their kin. They look forward to sharing their bounties, and they make sure that everyone is fed. They share their feelings without reservation, listen wholeheartedly to each other, and respect differing opinions. Though each family member's privacy is respected, no one is barred from anyone's rooms, and no one engages in forced entry. All take pride in their home and willingly put forth effort to keep it clean and beautiful. In such a home, the occupants are guided by the following credo from the philosopher Soren Kierkegaard: ". . . to love human beings is still the only thing worth living for—without that love, you really do not live."[1]

It is understandable that many people will reject what has just been described as a fairy tale. After all, there is no precedent for it. Their thinking has been deeply influenced by their attachment to the idea that humanity should be divided. Thus many people will oppose the new ideas and those who hold them, perhaps even resorting to violence and persecution. Some learned skeptics may brand such views of the future world as "utopian," pointing to a list of short-lived nineteenth-century utopian communities in North America: the New Harmony commune, the Oneida Community, the Amana Society, the Separatist Society of Zoar, and the Shakers.

But were their efforts really failures? I don't think so. Their aborted efforts were a sign of developing enlightenment. The spark of hope within the people who founded these communities had broken into a flame, and they were inspired to attempt to put into action what great thinkers of the past had only dreamed of doing. Their communities were stepping-stones to future successes. That is progress.

Such experiments in community living show a conviction among sensitive, hopeful people that undesirable conditions can be improved; that humans have the capacity to improve those conditions; and that they have the right to live in a community where freedom, justice, and equality reign—where poverty, homelessness, and social or spiritual corruption find no home. These experiments also demonstrated that there were people who had the will and fortitude to implement their vision. In a way, they expressed a social impulse that continues to grow stronger in the face of considerable resistance from reactionary forces that fear progressive change.

A Matter of Time

This impulse will effloresce when humanity recognizes its familyhood and unites. It is not a matter of whether this will ever transpire, but rather a matter of when it will happen, for it is divinely ordained. Christians, whether they realize it or not, are expected to share this belief, for their sacred scriptures feature the Lord's prayer: ". . . Thy Kingdom come, Thy will be done on Earth as it is in Heaven." That implies a promise from God that there will come a time when all human beings will have internalized the principle of the oneness of humankind. It will be a time when the term "the children of God" will be profoundly meaningful to most people. With a deeper understanding of the term and all that it implies, people will be reticent to hold grudges and reluctant to engage in cheating, arguing, or fighting with anyone. They will try earnestly to become effective advocates for unity in their communities. Their greatest source of joy will come from serving others.

The impulse to create the ideal society has long been evident. In some individuals, the impulse has been a catalyst for change and an inspiration to dream about inculcating possibilities that could transform that which is ineffective into something that is effective. In the fifth century B.C., Plato described in *The Republic* a society that would be ruled by philosophers and in which the virtues of justice and wisdom would prevail. During the English Renaissance two great thinkers, Thomas More and Francis Bacon, revealed their ideas about what would make society more equitable and efficient. Both More's *Utopia* (1516) and Bacon's *New Atlantis* (1627) described societies that, while imperfect, were in the process of advancing toward perfection. They reveal a pragmatic, commonsense guide to traversing the pathway to perfection.[2]

Many other writers, philosophers, and scientists, concerned with the state of the human condition and sensing humankind's untapped potential for social and spiritual growth, have revealed in writing the course they believe should be taken to create the ideal society. There seems to be among most people a spark of hope that somehow their situation and that of their community will improve—that there will come a time when whatever it is that plagues them will cease to exist. Though confronted by personal, local, and global crises on a regular basis, and having to wrestle with doubts from time to time, that spark of hope has not vanished. Nevertheless, they refrain from sharing that feeling for fear of being denounced as a foolish dreamer, a radical, or a disrupter of the existing order. So they keep quiet and wait, continually struggling to avoid becoming dispirited.

The great English poet Alfred Tennyson was not quiet and was unwilling to wait. He knew that what he envisioned would someday materialize. He sensed in the mid-nineteenth century the same thing that the rash of utopian communities were sensing in that period of great expectancy: the impulse that is driving humanity toward unity. This is evident in his poem "Locksley Hall," which tells of a future that will emerge after nations have spent themselves in the futility of modern warfare:

Till the war-drum throbbed no longer, and
the battle-flags were furled
In the Parliament of Man, the Federation
of the world.[3]

To Tennyson, it was obvious that national convulsions of war would be a part of the evolutionary process that would eventually result in a world federation whose inhabitants would function as family members. Some contemporary critics would classify Tennyson's vision as utopian.

It is unfortunate that "utopia" is equated in most circles today with an impractical well-meaning concept that cannot be actualized. The trouble is that humanity faces the choice of either continuing to make the best of a worsening situation—and we know where that can lead us—or striving to find or create a more just society in which the social, economic, and spiritual ills that afflict us can be successfully addressed. Actually, we do not seem to have much of a choice, for to align ourselves with the process of decline is to pursue a disastrous route headed toward increased and prolonged suffering that needlessly delays the advancement of civilization. By focusing on the process of unification and growth and aligning ourselves with organizations that promote oneness and unity, we will notice the signs of progress and the encouraging possibilities. An evolutionary pattern, drawn and guided by the Divine Hand, becomes apparent.

CHAPTER 11

GLOBAL UNIFICATION

When we trace the social evolution of humankind, we cannot help but come to the conclusion that humanity's next logical step is global unification—a step that would mark the fulfillment of humanity's destiny. It is certain that families of the past who continually fought against one another and vowed they would never stop hating one another never dreamed they would one day come together as members of the same clan and swear allegiance to it. The clans resorted to the same feuding behavior as the families before them, banding together as tribes; and the tribes followed the same pattern of resistance as did the clans before coming together to form nations. Today, as the twin processes of growth and decline, unification and disintegration accelerate, they are exposing the nation-state's inability to cope with the mounting unprecedented international pressures and problems. It is becoming apparent that it is time we take the next step.

It is interesting to note that with each surge forward in our social evolution we human beings have developed more advanced attitudinal and behavioral characteristics—characteristics and outlooks that people of past generations would have deemed impossible. As movement from the nation-state to world federation forges ahead, more people than ever before are shedding provincial attitudes and embracing world initiatives such as world trade and developing a desire to help those in desperate need who live thousands of miles away. People are breaking away from traditional religious systems and adopting broader spiritual beliefs. Today people are more tolerant than those who lived in the nineteenth century, when signs of globalization were not apparent to the generality of humankind, when nationalism reigned. The development of these advanced characteristics was due to the discovery and acceptance of realities that eluded past generations. In time, the new knowledge inspired people to alter their attitudes and behavior, and as a result, their outlook broadened.

For example, when tribes were united into nations, people, in time, took on nationalistic characteristics, demonstrating greater allegiance to their country than to their tribe. In fact, the assimilation of the tribes was so thorough that many of them have little influence in the way people think and behave. When people in general finally recognize that all are members of the same human family, we will have a different outlook than most of us do today. We will be aware of aspects of reality that have eluded the generality of humankind ever since the first Homo sapiens appeared. We will know that the Earth is our common home. Not only will we view everyone on the planet as a family member; our understanding of the true nature of humankind will heighten our instinct to love and protect all of our family members. As a result, whomever we meet—regardless of social station, education, culture, religion, vocation, or profession—will be embraced as a brother or sister. No preference will be given to the sophisticated over the seemingly primitive. We will recognize all as children of God, striving to focus on the good, not the faults of our family members. As a consequence, ridicule and humiliation, even cynicism will fade away, as will suspicion. Trust will reign. Love will be expressed more openly by both men and women and reciprocated in kind. Men will be unafraid to cry, because they will have developed those spiritual qualities such as tenderness, compassion, and gentleness that most men in the 1900s felt were female characteristics. Each person will become a force for unity in their community. Our greater appreciation of diversity will stem from our wholehearted embrace of oneness, for differences will be viewed as springing from a single organic unit, much like the branches of a tree. What is commonly referred to as interracial marriage today will not be viewed as such in the future. We will not be identified according to the color of our skin; the terms "Black" and "White" will not be used. We will all be committed to eliminating every trace of injustice from our community.

Human relationships will improve. The concept of "stranger" will become obsolete. We will think of those whom we do not know as long lost brothers or sisters. The more different their appearance from ours, the more appreciated they will be. We will greet them with enthusiasm, not suspicion. If they have a need, our first impulse will be to help them. We will be more courteous and thoughtful toward each other, more willing to go out of our way to do others a favor, to bring them pleasure. We will seek opportunities to serve.

We will find far more joy in serving others than in attaining material goods. Giving, rather than taking, will become our first impulse. Power will be viewed not as an instrument of control, dominance, and influence, but as an opportunity to serve others. Those who are most powerful will be those who serve the most. We will be guided by a spiritual principle that goes a step beyond the Golden Rule, preferring others over ourselves. When this principle is sincerely practiced, there will be no chance of developing pride in performing acts of service, for the more we serve, the more humble we will become. Whatever pleasure is derived from serving others will come from knowing that we have made their lives a little more secure. Their happiness will make us happier, knowing that service to others pleases God will be our greatest source of joy. With that awareness, we will have an incentive to continue to be of service to humankind. In our interactions with others we will counter hate with love and thoughts of war with thoughts of peace.

In the future global society, women will enjoy full partnership with men in all fields of endeavor, while men will discover within themselves capacities that were once considered part of the female makeup. Men will find joy in being more tenderhearted, more nurturing, more understanding, and more patient. They will listen to what women have to say with an open mind and a new respect. As a consequence, it will be an age less masculine and more permeated with feminine ideals. In other words, human beings will have a more balanced outlook on life, no longer resorting to the kinds of behavior that have led to so much mayhem and misery when women had no voice in shaping policies and modes of behavior. This social arrangement will lead to a more peaceful, compassionate world. The rush to settle disputes violently will no longer prevail. When disputes arise, the immediate instinct will be to develop bridges of understanding between squabbling individuals, institutions, or communities because everyone will be more nurturing and aware of their relatedness. With that kind of collective thinking, a moral and psychological climate will be created in which international peace can emerge and become permanently rooted.

Practices such as female genital mutilation, wife-beating, and other brutal methods men have used to keep women "in their place" will no longer be practiced.

With the knowledge that everyone is related, we will view every child in the community as a family member. As a consequence, we will feel obligated whenever we encounter a child to cheer her heart, to make whatever time is spent with her a joyous occasion. With such an attitude, teachers will adopt the role of classroom parent, and parents will adopt the role of teacher when the child is at home. Both will consult regularly, exchanging insights about the child whom they are teaching. Educators will not view their students as economic resources, but rather as human beings who have the right to learn about their humanness. To achieve that end, teachers will strive to discover, release, and develop the mental, physical, and spiritual potentialities of their students, who will be seen as young family members. With such an understanding, teachers will be more committed to doing the very best job possible and will help children become acquainted with their true selves—a necessary step in finding the path that constitutes the journey of life. Children will be taught why it is important to stay the course and how to keep from straying. As a result, children will gain a deep appreciation for discipline and order.

Hatred of anyone because of their skin color, age, gender, or religion will be so abnormal that it will be viewed by society as a mental illness. Special remedies will be used to heal the malady. Humility will be highly prized, whereas egotism and selfishness will be looked upon as emotional defects.

Effects on Education

The principle of the oneness of humankind will be integrated into the school curriculum and reflected in every course a child takes from kindergarten through the twelfth grade. Teaching the oneness of humankind in school will be a vaccine against the disease of racism. Education will reflect a broader and deeper view of our planet and the life upon it than has been offered by educators influenced by the prevailing fractured view of humanity. Students will view each other as family members and as world citizens; they will be more globally conscious than we are today. As a consequence, they will want to work together with their fellow students in the pursuit of knowledge. Whatever they unearth, they will willingly share with others. There will be no hoarding of knowledge as a means of flaunting one's sense of superiority. They will look upon their schooling, first and foremost, as an opportunity to prepare themselves to help make the world a better place. It will be very obvious to them that the planet Earth is their real country, their basic home. As a result, when people are suffering in another part of the planet, the students will be moved to do something to help their family members thousands of miles away. Their urge will lead to a constructive plan of action, and carrying out the plan will bring them joy. They will have a greater desire to maintain the balance of nature and keep our skies and waterways free of pollution. What will drive the desire is their awareness of the need to keep their planet as healthy as possible for their brothers and sisters and for future family members. They will want to do something to prevent diminishing plant and animal species from becoming extinct. They will learn about certain aspects of reality that children of previous generations were unaware of: that ours is a nonlinear world; that all things are interrelated; that all life is precious; that there is a reason for everything that happens, even the falling of a leaf. They will view science as a servant of humankind and not the other way around. They will no longer pursue sciences that begin and end in words; instead, they will study sciences that will help them contribute to the advancement of humankind, their greater family. They will look forward to involvement in community service projects, which will be viewed by educators as having as much value as mathematics or chemistry. In order to ensure that they will be able to feed, clothe, and house themselves, and not be dependent on others, they will learn a vocational skill. Everyone, regardless of economic and social status, will have an opportunity to pursue an education from kindergarten to postgraduate university-level study. One's ability to meet tuition fees will not be a factor.

Education will offer students a sound understanding of the purpose of life, an awareness of who they are and the nature of the human being. Such an education will develop in its students a deep appreciation for all forms of life, inculcating an awareness of Earth's place and purpose in the universe. Students will learn how to work in groups, as well as how to use consultation to settle disputes and solve problems. They will develop such a love for knowledge that they will become lifelong seekers of the truth. They will learn how to rely on their intuition as well as reason in solving problems and exploring the vast unknown for new knowledge. Gaining new understanding will not only become a source of great pleasure, it will offer an opportunity for sharing with others what one has gleaned, heightening the pleasure.

Schoolteachers will be highly valued, considered one of the most essential members of the community. Securing a job as a teacher will not be as easy as it is today, for, while maintaining high scores in their university work will be important, the emphasis will be on the prospective teacher's character and ability to communicate effectively, especially with children. Most important will be the teacher's love for people and their ability to communicate lovingly. A self-centered straight-"A" student will be considered a potential detriment to children and will not be allowed in the classroom as a teacher. The ideal teacher must be highly developed spiritually in addition to being properly trained, creative, and learned.

Teachers of the future will understand that human nature is fundamentally spiritual; they will focus attention on helping youngsters to grow spiritually as well as intellectually; they will help to discover, release, and develop each child's human potential; they will know how to help a youngster develop the precious properties of her or his soul; they will know how to get students involved in community service projects; they will know how to integrate the oneness of humankind into a curriculum; they will help students think more creatively and deeply; they will be able to use their intuition to reach and teach students; they will know how to help students overcome feelings of inferiority; they will know how to motivate and inspire students, and will help them set and achieve personal and career objectives and goals.

The university schools of education that prepare students to become educators will have abandoned all courses based on the old notion that humanity was meant to be a divided body. Prospective teachers and administrators will enter the profession with an understanding of the realities underlying the principle of the oneness of humankind, and the courses they design will reflect that understanding. They will know how racism develops and how to heal those who have been affected by it. They will know how to draw parents into the process of educating their children and will be equipped to train parents in carrying out their educational responsibilities as parents.

In the future, regardless of our scholastic achievements, we will not be considered truly educated if we are unaware of our physical, mental, or spiritual potentialities. One of the requirements for graduation from school will be a demonstrated awareness of our potentialities and active involvement in developing them. This is most important, because gaining an understanding of our potentialities and developing them enables us to gain an understanding of our true self. When we neglect this responsibility, we allow whatever stimuli may be around us to fashion our personality and shape our character. By doing so, we run the risk of becoming slaves to convention, never experiencing real freedom.

Economic Implications

Those involved in the economy in the future, whether farmer, factory worker, manager, lawyer, or doctor, will view their job responsibilities as opportunities to make the world a better place. With that committed sense, workers will view themselves as community builders, playing a role in safeguarding the security of their community and their employer as well. After all, successful commerce is an essential element of a community's welfare. Without it, poverty and all of its hope-sapping deprivations will result. Workers will, therefore, take on the responsibility of assuring that their communities remain free of poverty by striving for excellence in the work place. Imagine a workforce composed of people believing that they are all related, finding pleasure in serving one another, all striving for excellence because they believe it is necessary for the creation and maintenance of a healthy community.

Those who are poor will not be in that condition because they have not tried to find employment. In such a situation the community will be obligated to assist the person, and the assistance will not be offered grudgingly; it will be offered with love. As a consequence, those receiving assistance will not be stigmatized in any way.

While material gain will be secondary, all will be assured of an adequate income. Because everyone in the workplace will have internalized the principle of oneness, they will not view their coworkers as competitors for a promotion. On the contrary, they will view them as family members and will be dedicated to supporting one another. When someone receives a promotion, it will be greeted by others with sincere happiness. The jealousy and envy that are so prevalent in today's workplace will find no place. A spirit of altruism will drive the work effort, for work will be seen as a spiritual exercise. The same attitude manifested in one's place of worship will be manifested within the workplace and everywhere else. Whatever services a person renders will be influenced by the belief that work done in the spirit of service is the highest form of worship. This attitude will make the employee an on-the-job peacemaker and unifier. The backbiting, rumor mongering, character assassination, and cutthroat political maneuvering that are so prevalent in the workplace today will be recognized as community-damaging practices of the past. Workers will have no inclination to resort to those practices and will, in fact, find the very thought of them repugnant.

The business climate will be so pleasing that workers will look forward to reporting for work. Thus absenteeism will cease to be a problem. Labor-management conflict will be a thing of the past. When supervisors and rank-and-file workers view each other as family members, there will be a natural tendency to cooperate, to support one another, to work together for the common good. There will be no need for strikes. Whatever differences arise will be handled by a board composed of diverse membership, relying on consultation to forge its decisions. During the consultative process, all participants will focus on what is best for the group and will avoid promoting personal interests or reputations. In consulting, the supervisor and rank-and-file worker will have an equal voice.

While private ownership will exist, owners will respect and appreciate the contributions their employees make toward maintaining a successful commercial enterprise. To ensure that everyone benefits from the collective effort, everyone will share in the company's profits. This will make everyone a partial owner, which will reinforce their loyalty to the company, which views itself as a contributor to the welfare of the community. Because it will be recognized that owners have taken risks in starting businesses, their share in the profits will naturally be greater than that of a rank-and-file worker, but the difference will not be extreme.

In fact, in the future global society, extremes of wealth and poverty will no longer exist, for the gap between the rich and poor will be considerably narrowed. Homelessness, famine, illiteracy, and medical neglect will not be a problem. There will be no billionaires, no chief executives receiving end-of-the year bonuses of ten million dollars or more after laying off hundreds of employees; such practices will be considered sinful. Statistics such as the top five percent of Americans in 1997 possess more than 60 percent of all household wealth will be a thing of the past.[1] Such conditions will not exist because the population, believing that they are all family members, will not allow such an imbalance. The instinct to give and share will be greater than the desire to take and keep. In order to have more time for family and spiritual development, the work week will be reduced to no more than thirty-two hours.

Diminishing Crime Rates and Social Problems

When humanity internalizes the reality of the oneness of humankind, crime rates will diminish. Punching someone in the nose will become so rare that it will be considered as reprehensible as murder is today. Drug problems will be nonexistent, and the consumption of liquor will be greatly reduced because there will be no reason to use either. With a healthy understanding of the purpose of one's life, there will be no need to escape from life's challenges. With no serious drug and alcohol problem, monies normally used to treat the multitude of social problems associated with drug abuse and addiction will be funneled into areas such as education, medical research, and care for the elderly.

There will be little or no tax evasion, because paying one's taxes will be seen as a privilege—an opportunity to assist the needy and help one's extended family stay healthy. Theft and burglary will be rare because no one will want to steal from a family member. Arson will become a thing of the past for the same reason that stealing will be such a rare occurrence. The absence of competition in the workplace will put an end to white-collar crime. Con-artistry, extortion, and illegal scams will disappear because such practices are normally directed toward strangers, a social classification that will no longer exist. With very little crime, there will be no need for the extended network of prisons and youth correctional institutions, and the court system will be greatly reduced. Courts will devote most of their time to promoting healing rather than meting out punishment. The law will be spiritually based. Police will spend most of their time in crime prevention education, maintaining vehicular traffic, settling intra- and intercommunity disputes, and assisting survivors of natural or man-made disasters. Instead of being feared, the police will be revered.

The Role of the Media

The media will garner a new respect. No longer influenced by vested interest groups, it will be dedicated to uplifting the spirit of the community and enhancing the spiritual, emotional, and mental development of the individual. Movies, plays, and radio and television programming will be designed to strengthen the moral base of society and support community unity. Newspapers, magazines, radio, and television will take seriously their responsibility to pursue the truth relentlessly, never succumbing to pressure from the outside to halt or slow down the pursuit. Journalists will avoid judging newsmakers and institutions, who will continually sharpen their skills at unearthing evidence and appraising it, communicating their findings as clearly as possible. Journalists will view themselves as servants of the community, never bowing to manipulation and trickery of any kind while unearthing the truth. Whatever they do professionally will be driven by the desire to uphold the profession's spiritually based standards to the fullest. Cooperation with fellow journalists will be commonplace. There will be no need or desire to resort to sensationalism or using one's position to solicit favors. The pursuit of excellence will be driven by a deep desire to please God, not to impress coworkers and competitors.

Health Care

Today's cutthroat competition and prejudices in the realm of health care will not exist. Medical doctors, chiropractors, naturopaths, homeopaths, acupuncturists, and folkloric healers will appreciate one another's services and will work together to provide the best care possible for the community. They will also engage in transdisciplinary research. Because all people will view each other as relatives, the energy-sapping immune-depleting stress that plagues contemporary men and women will be considerably reduced. Trust will have replaced suspicion. More emphasis will be placed on interpersonal cooperation instead of competition. This will have a salubrious effect on individuals and communities. Stress-related diseases will be a rarity. A unified healing community comprised of disciplines that are presently at odds with one another will cooperate in eliminating diseases like cancer and multiple sclerosis. There will be a universally developed consciousness on the part of most people to maintain a healthy body and mind through diet, exercise, and such meditative practices as yoga and tai chi. It will be common knowledge that there is a correlation between actively engaging in a spiritual development regimen and maintaining sound health. Because the use of tobacco, narcotics, and alcohol will be practically nonexistent, there will be far less emphysema, cyrrhosis of the liver, lung cancer, AIDS, heart disease, and injuries sustained from automobile accidents resulting from drunken driving. Living to the age of one hundred or more will be commonplace.

A "United States of the World"

With a global awareness of the oneness of humankind, people will see the necessity for the nations of the world to come together as a federation. There will be one nation—a sort of "United States of the World," if you will. Nations that exist today will become states in this planetary government, whose constitution will be spiritually based, reflecting the need for all individuals to understand and fulfill their purpose in life, and guaranteeing their right of expression as well as their right to work, vote, worship, and receive free medical care. Such a federation will ensure freedom from hunger and protection from all forms of oppression and terrorism. It will view racial prejudice, religious prejudice, and gender prejudice as crimes and will provide guidelines as to how these crimes are to be treated. While the constitution will outlaw war, it will provide for the establishment and maintenance of a world police force that will swing into action should a tyrant state rise to threaten another state. In such cases, all of the states in the federation would be obligated to join forces in putting down the threat.

Every state will contribute in manpower or material resources to the police force.

While the primary responsibility of the planetary government will be to maintain the unity of the human family, it will also insure that personal freedoms and individual initiative will be safeguarded. It will be guided by the principle of unity in diversity, not uniformity. The government will have legislative, judicial, and executive branches. Those who are elected to the world legislature will view themselves as trustees of all of humankind. They will not be beholden to those who elect them, nor to any vested interest group or political party. There will be no political parties because they will be recognized as engines of disunity, breeding grounds of corruption. Lobbying will be forbidden as well, for it will be seen as a cause of partisanship, which leads to destructive factionalism and distrust. Whatever elected members do will be influenced by their genuine desire to serve their fellow human beings' best interests and to do everything possible to maintain the unity of the human family.

It is important to note that in the future global society the various elected officials will look upon each other neither as strangers nor as allies promoting a particular agenda, but rather as members of the same family, dedicated to its unification. Their outlook toward their responsibilities will be markedly different than that of today's elected officials. They will not be motivated by the need to seek reelection, the desire for popularity, the need to curry favor with influential individuals or institutions, or the need to promote their own ideas over everyone else's. In fact, such drives will be considered immoral. For the most part, elected officials will be united in thought and purpose. Their reliance on prayer and their deep understanding of divinely revealed behavioral principles will determine the actions they take. In electing the members of the world parliament, voters will seek

out those women and men whose spiritual development and moral character are exemplary. Their record of service will also be sought out and carefully reviewed.

The global executive body will oversee the various agencies that are responsible for operating, among other things, the planet's transportation
and communication infrastructure. They will also be responsible for man-
aging the planet's natural resources, maintaining a dynamic health service
that will afford the best medical treatment for all, regardless of income.
Other agencies will deal with other areas of public concern such as education, ecology, disaster relief, and a world security force. The executive council
will work in concert with parliament in drafting a plan of some duration
that is designed to meet the social, economic, educational, transportation,
communication, moral, unific, and health needs of the inhabitants of Earth.
Each state within the federation will have a set of goals that is meant to care
for its particular needs. A council agency will have the responsibility of
finding out what are the needs of each state. It will work closely with the
states in fashioning their goals. The term of service of the executive council
will be long enough to assure the fulfillment of the goals of its plan.

Monies derived from a global graduate income tax system will finance
the work of the executive council and parliament. As I mentioned earlier
there will be no tax evasion problems, for people will be basically altruistic,
and find pleasure in knowing that what they contribute in the way of taxes
is helping the needy, family members who are having tests and difficulties.
Knowing that the tax-money will be used to maintain an orderly, united
and peaceful world will also be a source of assurance. While a council agency
will be responsible for collecting the taxes, the majority of the money collected will be funneled to local communities. The rationale being—without a solid foundation a house will crumble.

A world court, appointed by the Executive Council, will adjudicate disputes between states and global civil and criminal cases. Those working for the court will be dedicated pursuers of justice, and not seekers of legalized revenge.

Local, regional, and state elections of their respective governing councils will take place annually. All citizens will want to vote because of their genuine interest in the health of their community. Like the election of the world parliament, all local, regional, and state elections will be held by secret ballot. There will be no electioneering or campaigning of any kind. In electing council members, voters will take into account a person's spiritual development and strength of character. Those who seek office either subtly or overtly will not be elected, for humility will be a necessary quality in any elected official. The council members will employ consultation as a means of arriving at decisions. All council members will be working at internalizing the principle of preferring others over one's self. Their dedication to serving the community will stem from a sincere love of God. They will know that by loving God, they will be the recipient of God's love, which will come in the form of guidance in living one's life. Imagine what a council can achieve if all of its members are sincerely seeking guidance from The Source of all knowledge and love.

People's view of power will be different than our present-day view of power, which can be purchased, seized, transferred or inherited. Today it is thought of as something that can be secured from someone else, or somewhere else. Power will have nothing to do with control or dominance. Service to one's fellow human beings will be viewed as power. The most powerful people will be those who serve the most. Only God will judge who has attained that station.

The council will have legislative, judicial and executive powers, as well as the responsibility to create and maintain unity and harmony and economic prosperity in the community. Special agencies will be set up to help the council carry out its responsibilities.

No council member on any level will have any authority. Only the institution of which he or she is a part will have authority. A spokesman of the council will express the view of the institution, not his own. The citizenry will take an active part in the community governance by offering recommendations and advice at regular town meetings. Citizens will offer suggestions on how to improve the people's quality of life, improve the system of governance, and strengthen the economy. At this forum people will volunteer their services to the council.

The local council will look forward to receiving the citizens' suggestions, giving them serious consideration. The community's contribution will be considered a reliable reservoir of fresh ideas that will make the council's work more fruitful and efficient. In consequence, the council will continually encourage the citizenry to continue to offer recommendations and advice. Cooperation between the council and citizenry will lead to a trusting relationship and a common understanding that the governance of the community is everyone's responsibility. Such cooperation will be ensured by the common understanding that all are related. A spirit of familyhood will permeate the consultation chamber. The fact that everyone is engaged in developing his or her spiritual potentialities will be a safeguard against dissension and factionalism.

The Emergence of a World Culture

While the United States of the World is being firmly established, there will be a blending of characteristics of the national cultures, along with new qualities that usually result when groups are in the process of merging. In other words, a world culture will evolve. The formation of a world culture doesn't mean that people will be forced to abandon their ethnic culture. No one will be forced to change their life styles. Whatever changes occur will result from personal choice and consultation with others. In a sense, it will be comparable to the way the American culture is developing today. No new American is forced to give up his or her ethnic culture. In time, however, her children will have less of an attachment to her ethnic culture, and will be influenced more by the American culture she has freely embraced. Viewing oneself as a world citizen is an important step to embracing the world culture. In time, a practicing world citizen finds himself happily immersed in the world culture and proudly identifies himself with it.

In the future, when people everywhere will have embraced the fact that they are related to one another, it will be easier for them to recognize that there is only one God. When we finally internalize the true meaning of the statement that every human being is a child of God, it will be clear that, just as there is only one God, only one human family, and one country, there is—and always has been—only one religion, the religion of God. This realization will eventually seem obvious and logical to all.

The Process of Divine Education

While traditional organized religion is terribly fractured today, there is among a few religious and philosophical leaders who openly express their belief in the oneness of humankind, a growing understanding that all major faiths have common spiritual and social aims and, perhaps, similar roots. The present Dalai Lama is one of those religious leaders:

I maintain that every major religion of the world—Buddhism, Christianity, Confucianism, Hinduism, Islam, Jainism, Sikhism, Taoism,

Zoroastrianism—has similar ideals of love, the same goal of benefiting humanity through spiritual practice, and the same effect of making their followers into better human beings. All religions teach moral precepts for perfecting the functions of the mind, body and speech. All teach us not to lie or steal or take others' lives, and so on.

All religions agree upon the necessity to control the undisciplined mind that harbors selfishness and other roots of trouble, and each teaches a path leading to a spiritual state that is peaceful, disciplined, ethical, and wise. It is this sense that I believe all religions have essentially the same message. Differences of dogma may be ascribed to differences of time and circumstance as well as cultural influences; indeed, there is no end to scholastic argument when we consider the purely meta-physical side of religion. However, it is much more beneficial to try to implement in daily life the shared precepts for goodness taught by all religions rather than to argue about minor differences in approach.[2]

The Historian Arnold Toynbee also sees the same divine vein running through all of the world's major religions. He alludes to their oneness:

> At first sight, Buddhism, Christianity and Islam and Judaism may appear to be very different from each other. But when you look be-neath the surface, you will find that all of them are addressing them-selves primarily to the individual psyche or soul; they are trying to persuade it to overcome its own self-centeredness and they are offering it the means for achieving this. They all find the same remedy. They all teach that egocentricity can be conquered by love.[3]

When we are able to cut through the religious dogma and ritual that have led to sectarian exclusivity, we will see the thread of oneness running through the heart of the world's great religions. Drawing their inspiration from the same Source, they have much in common. Our Supreme Parent has always been consistent in his desires for our behavior toward each other. In reality, all religions are one, connected like links in a chain.

Unfortunately, from the beginning we have been unable to see this divine linkage, just as we have been unable to recognize the oneness of humankind. Much brainpower has been generated over the centuries toward creating and legitimizing humanity's fractured view of itself and of religion. Our view of one has reinforced the other, forming the prevailing notions about the structure of humanity and about religion, thus guiding our spiritual and social development.

Accelerating Change

As we enter the twenty-first century, we can anticipate acceleration in the process of unification in every phase of life. Though we do not know exactly what events will quicken the pace, they will occur as inevitably as they have in the past, but this time with greater rapidity and impact. Changes will take place that people in the past would have considered impossible to materialize.

We do not have to go back very far to appreciate this point. In 1900, not even the most erudite and powerful of individuals knew of the progress that would be made toward drawing the human family together in the twentieth century. It was a time when the horse and buggy were the primary forms of transportation. In America, Jim Crowism had replaced slavery as a means of keeping African-Americans in an inferior social standing. The lynching of blacks was considered an act of chivalry by those who carried out the hangings. The Ku Klux Klan was glorified by the news media and powerful politicians in both the South and the North. Imperial colonialism was enjoying its heyday. China, the most populated country in the world, had been carved up and ruled by a number of European powers. India, with the second largest population, was one of the shining jewels in the British Crown. Child labor was commonplace; sweatshops abounded. Indoor plumbing was a luxury, as were the electric light and the telephone. Women were second-class citizens. The idea of television and manned missions into outer space were nothing more than far-fetched themes for science fiction writers.

Eighteen years into the new century, a tragic event—World War I—forced the world's political leaders to come together to create an international mechanism that would, they hoped, settle geopolitical disputes and put an end to war. While the League of Nations failed, it heightened humanity's awareness of the need for an international body that would have the power to establish and maintain world peace. An idea was born that would eventually grow into a global passion.

The passion was the result of World War II, the most destructive and ferocious war in human history, killing more than forty million people. When it was over, people everywhere clamored for a lasting peace. The United Nations came into being. Its Declaration of Human Rights fostered a greater consciousness of human equity and personal freedoms. A more vigorous and united effort to end racism, classism, and sexism resulted. International agencies were formed to elevate social justice everywhere. A global economy developed. Nations began pooling their resources for the common good. The United Nations forged an armed force to put down one nation's aggression toward another nation. There was a growing sense that the world was coming together. Through television, disasters in one part of the world evoked sympathy from people living thousands of miles away. Volunteerism mushroomed. Through the Internet, the networking and interconnection between individuals and communities geographically far apart and isolated was accelerated.

In a span of one hundred years much of humanity has shed primitive and divisive notions of reality and is now heading, whether it realizes it or not, toward even greater revelations. More and more people will recognize the need to work diligently to divest ourselves of our emotional attachments to falsehoods we have assumed to be the truth. Liberated from that stranglehold, we will gain a clearer vision of what God expects of us. We will realize that we—all six billion of us—are truly God's children and will learn to appreciate and love our brothers and sisters. Once that is learned, we will experience a joy that will stimulate the desire to work tirelessly to create the kind of worldwide society that God wants for us. We will know that his willingness to help us is constant. Collectively beseeching his assistance with purity of heart, we will receive the energy, the creativity, the determination and stamina to establish his Kingdom on Earth.

It is only a matter of time until this will happen. How long it takes depends upon when and how many of us will align ourselves with the process of unification that is already in constant motion. Promoting the principle of oneness will not be easy, especially in an atmosphere of doubt and fear of the unknown and untried. It will be doubly difficult when those who are skeptical and fearful are also sincere and well-meaning people. We will not want to offend them or hurt their feelings; we won't want to force anything upon anyone. It will be a dilemma because we will know how important it is for as many people as possible to discover, understand, and internalize this reality. This is essential to the establishment and maintenance of world peace. Knowledge alone will not ensure success in sharing the oneness of humanity with others. Faith is needed—the kind of faith the prophet Isaiah manifested so long ago:

> He shall judge between the nations, and shall decide for many peoples; and they shall beat their swords into plowshares, and their spears into pruning hooks; nation shall not lift up sword against nation, neither shall they learn war any more. . . .[4]

The fulfillment of Isaiah's prophecy is dependent on humanity's awakening to the reality of the oneness of humankind. His was not the only divine voice that proclaimed the coming of a time of great peace. There have been reminders throughout the centuries, including appeals for the family of man to live in harmony and concord.

Humanity has had difficulty taking those appeals to heart. The record is abundantly clear: Humanity has taken a course that is opposite from the course it has been advised to take. The results have dimmed the light of hope, turning the hopeful into skeptics.

But today that light is brightening, for modern science corroborates what the divines of the past have proclaimed time and time again: that all human beings are members of one family. Our greatest challenge will not be the establishment of world peace and a just economy, but rather taking the step that is absolutely necessary in order to establish a lasting peace and a just economy—uniting the human family. For that to happen, recognition and the internalization of the reality of the oneness of humankind must take place on a global scale.

This can be achieved, for all of us, regardless of educational attainments, are endowed with the capacity to love and to serve one another, two essential prerequisites to unifying a community. That this has never been done before does not mean it cannot be done. There has never been a time when the need for unity was more apparent. For the first time, science and religion are in agreement about a reality that has been rejected for far too long.

True freedom will be realized when we make the effort to embrace that reality. Once that happens, we will see in the face of everyone we meet the sign of our Creator, and that will inspire us to love and serve whomever we know or meet. We stand at the threshold of hope. So that we may see clearly what is before us—the pathway to peace—we must lift our hearts to the process of unification and remain steadfastly focused on what it will lead to: a united, more spiritually grounded world, where oneness is as real as the air we breathe.

NOTES

2 / A Fractured View of Humanity

1. Zinn, p. 515.
2. Rutstein, *Racism: Unraveling the Fear,* p. 95.
3. Zinn, pp. 129, 130.
4. Davenport, p. 23.
5. Wilson, pp. 49–53, 204, 205.
6. Walvin, p. 13.
7. Takaki, pp. 39, 40.
8. Conrad, p. 34.
9. See Hughes.
10. Lincoln, p. 40.
11. Lincoln, p. 42.
12. Bancroft, p. 87.
13. Bancroft, pp. 328, 329.
14. Bancroft, p. 329.
15. Conrad, p. 34.
16. Fishell and Quarels, pp. 114, 115.
17. Joy Leary, speech presented at a race unity conference at the University of Massachusetts, Amherst, Spring 1995.
18. Goodman, pp. 155, 156.
19. Thomas, p. 31.
20. Koch and Peden, p. 256.
21. Conner Cruise O'Brein, "Thomas Jefferson Radical and Racist," *Atlantic Monthly,* October 1996.
22. Zinn, pp.183, 184.
23. Fishell and Quarels, pp. 204, 205.
24. Aristotle, *Politics,* Book 1, Chapter 2; see also Starr, p. 17.
25. See Rousseau, Book 1, Chapter 2.
26. Fishell and Quarels, p. 82.
27. Kareem Abdul-Jabbar, p. 77.
28. Kareem Abdul-Jabbar, p. 77.
29. Haller, p. 4.
30. Cited in Smith, p. 32.
31. Popkin, p. 93.
32. Mazel, p. 32.
33. Conrad, pp. 102, 103.
34. Brandt, pp. 21–29.
35. Tiger Lionel, "Trump Race Card," *Wall Street Journal,* 23 February 1996.
36. Smith, p. 33
37. Smith, p. 33
38. Smith, p. 33
39. Smith, p. 33
40. Smith, p. 33
41. Smith, p. 34

42. Smith, p. 34
43. Smith, p. 34
44. Smith, p. 34
45. Smith, p. 34
46. Royce A. Rensberger, "A Look at Race Without the Old Labels," *Springfield Union News,* 3 February 1995, pp. 29–30.

47. Robert S. Boyd, "Scientists' Idea of Race Only Skin Deep," *Miami Herald,* 13 October 1996.
48. Rutstein and Morgan, pp. 232–33.

3 / Overcoming the Emotional Attachment to Ignorance

1. Loewen, p. 53.
2. Locke and Stern, pp. 441–45.
3. Barrett, p. 17.

4. Covey, p. 319.
5. Murchie, p. 238.
6. Mathew Fox, interview by Polly Baumer, *Many Hands,* Spring 1993, p. 2.

4 / Exposing the Myths

1. Zinn, pp. 183, 184.
2. Davis, p. 17.
3. Murchie, p. 351.
4. Griffiths, pp. 68, 69.
5. Griffiths, pp. 68, 69.
6. Rutstein and Morgan, pp. 232, 233.
7. Comas, p. 31.
8. Murchie, p. 351
9. Murchie, p. 348.
10. Loewen, p. 120.
11. Loewen, p. 131.
12. See pictures of African artifacts in Central America in Van Sertima, p. 97.
13. Murchie, p. 348.
14. Comas, p. 30.
15. Fishberg, p. 63.
16. *Encyclopaedia Britannica,* s. v. "Jews."
17. Fishberg, p. 181.
18, Koestler, p. 187.
19. Koestler, p. 19.
20. Montague, pp. 225, 226.
21. Fishberg, p. 33.
22. Starr, pp. 224, 225n.
23. Dobzhansky, pp. 75–77.

24. S. Lofti, "The Biological Basis of the Oneness of Humankind" (paper written for the Institute for the Healing of Racism, 1998), p. 6.
25. King, p. 130.
26. Weatherford, p. 182.
27. Weatherford, p. 183.
28. Weatherford, p. 186.
29. Wissler, pp. 11, 12.
30. Guzman, p. 13.
31. Weatherford, p. 135.
32. Franklin, p. 27.
33. Hyman, pp. 55, 56.
34. Bennett, p. 19.
35. Zinn, p. 26.
36. Zinn, p. 27.
37. George Pransky, "Anger," (Practical Psychology Audio Series, 1991), p. 2.
38. Thomas Sowell, "Ethnicity and IQ," in Fraser, p. 74.
39. Howard Gardner, quoted in Robert J. Sternberg, "What Should We Ask About Intelligence?" *The American Scholar,* vol. 65, no. 2 (Spring 1996): 2.

40. Rutstein, *Healing Racism in America,* p. 93.
41. C. Steele, "Race and the Schooling of Black Americans," *Atlantic Monthly,* April 1992.
42. John Woodall, "Racism as a Disease," in Rutstein and Morgan, p. 25.
43. Mazel. p. 69.
44. *NewsHour with Jim Lehrer,* "Music for the Brain," 10 November 1998.

45. Ronald Kotulak, "Learning How to Use the Brain" (paper presented at Brain Development in Young Children: New Frontiers of Research Conference, Chicago, 13 June 1996).
46. Smith, p. 35.
47. See B. Tizard, pp. 247–316, 1974, for a study of what society classifies Black, White, and mixed children in a British orphanage.

5 / Gender Equality

1. Ueland, p. 110.
2. Ueland, p. 108.
3. Ueland, pp. 119, 120.
4. Ueland, p. 120.
5. Pat Cahill, "Redefining Manhood," *Springfield Union-News,* April 7, 1999, p. C3.
6. Thomas Jefferson, quoted in Zinn, p. 116.
7. Steinem, p. 96.
8. 'Abdu'l-Bahá, *Promulgation of Universal Peace,* p. 375.

6 / A New Perspective on Who We Are and Where We Live

1. *The Senses,* "Understanding," Discovery Channel, March 20, 1999.
1. Chopra, pp. 48, 49.
2. See Murchie, p. 314.
3. Eisler, pp. 132, 133.
3. Capra, p. 47.
4. Capra, p. 87.
5. See Russell, pp. 24, 25.
6. Capra, pp. 284, 285.
8. See Murchie, p. 314.
7. See Capra, p. 73.
9. Thich Nhat Hanh, p. 45.
10. John Muir, quoted in Hakim, p. 128.
11. Leakey and Lewin, p. 7.
12. Murchie, p.346.

13. See Anthony Robbins, *Robbins International, Living Health,* audiocassette.
14. 'Abdu'l-Bahá, p. 53.
15. See Judith Hopper, "A New Germ Theory," *Atlantic Monthly,* February 1999, p. 48.
16. See Robert Kotulak, "Learning How to Use the Brain" (paper presented to the Brain Development in Young Children: New Frontiers for Research Policy and Practice Conference, Chicago, June 13, 1996), p. 3.
17. Kofi Annan, "What Do I Do to Make Things Better," *Parade Magazine,* 5 December 1998, p. 5.

7 / The Role of Religion

1. See *The World Book,* vol. I (Chicago, 1967), p. 215.
2. See Marius, pp. 235–43.
3. Eisler, p. 133
4. See Timothy 2:11–14.
5. Thomas Aquinas, quoted in Khan and Khan, p. 32.
6. Pagels, p. 69.
7. Fatima Mernissi, quoted in Khan and Khan, p. 34.
8. Increase Mather, quoted in Conrad, p. 34.
9. See Conrad, p. 33.
10. See Conrad, pp. 36–40.
11. Foner, p. 52.
12. See Fishel and Quarels, p. 129.
13. See Fishel and Quarels, p. 141.
14. Malachi 2:10.
15. The Jewish Song of Peace, quoted in Scholl, p. 99.
16. Mark 3:25.
17. John 10:16.
18. Quran 3:103–5.
19. An Islamic tradition, quoted in Scholl, p. 101.
20. Bhagavad Gita 6:29.
21. From the Hindu scriptures, quoted in Scholl, p. 100.
22. Jinasena, Adipurana.
23. Quoted in Moss, p.113.
24. Quoted in Moss, p.109.
25. Quoted in Moss, p. 113.
26. Bahá'u'lláh, *Gleanings,* p. 218.
27. Bahá'u'lláh, *The Kitáb-i-Aqdas,* p.16.

8 / Movements toward Peace

1. Pierre Teilhard de Chardin, in Scholl, p.104.
2. Erickson, p. 47.
3. Economist, Sept. 26, 1998, p. 59
4. White, p. 223.
5. Martin Buber, in Scholl, p. 105.

9 / An Emerging Pattern of Progress

1. See Kotulak, p. 1.
2. Alfred North Whitehead, quoted in Albert O. Hirschman, "A Rebuttal to Critics of Social Welfare," *Atlantic Monthly,* May 1989, p. 64.
3. Václav Havel, quoted in *New York Times,* 8 July 1994, OP ED page.
4. Teilhard de Chardin, p. 33.
5. Capra, pp. 28, 29, 46; Toynbee, p.117.

10 / The Coming of Age of Humanity

1. Keyes, p. 130.
2. Randolph Landry, "Dreamers of the Earth," *World Order,* Summer 1969, p. 14.
3. Landry, "Dreamers of the Earth," p. 15.

11 / Global Unification

1. Collins, Leondar, and Sklar, p. 6

2. Dalai Lama, p. 13.

3. Toynbee, p. 48.

4. Isaiah 2:4.

SELECTED
BIBLIOGRAPHY

'Abdu'l-Bahá. *Paris Talks: Addresses given by 'Abdu'l-Bahá in Paris in 1911–1912.* 11th ed. London: Bahá'í Publishing Trust, 1969.

_____. *The Promulgation of Universal Peace: Talks Delivered by 'Abdu'l-Bahá during His Visit to the United States and Canada in 1912.* Comp. Howard MacNutt. 2d ed. Wilmette, Ill.: Bahá'í Publishing Trust, 1982.

Abdul-Jabbar, Kareem. *Black Profiles of Courage.* New York: William Morrow, 1996.

Aristotle. *Politics.* Translated by Benjamin Jowett. Oxford: Claredon Press, 1916.

Bahá'u'lláh. *Gleanings from the Writings of Bahá'u'lláh.* 1st ps ed. Translated by Shoghi Effendi. Wilmette, Ill.: Bahá'í Publishing Trust, 1983.

_____. *The Kitáb-i-Aqdas: The Most Holy Book.* 1st ps ed. Wilmette, Ill.: Bahá'í Publishing Trust, 1993.

Baldwin, James. *The Evidence of Things Not Seen.* New York: Holt, Rinehart and Winston, 1995.

Bancroft, Fredric. *Slave Trading in the Old South.* Baltimore: J. H. Furst Company, 1931.

Barrett, David B., ed. *The World Christian Encyclopedia: A Comparative Survey of Churches and Religion in the Modern World, A.D. 1900 to 2000.* Nairobi: Oxford University Press, 1982.

Bennett, Lerone. *Before the Mayflower: A History of Black America.* Chicago: Johnson Company, 1982.

Bigelow, John, ed. *The Complete Works of Benjamin Franklin.* New York: G. P. Putnam and Sons, 1887.

Brandt, Allan. "Racism and Research: The Case of the Tuskegee Syphilis Study." Washington, D.C.: The Hastings Center Report, 1978.

Capra, Fritjof. *Turningpoint.* New York: Bantam, 1988.

Caton, Peggy, ed. *Equal Circles: Women and Men in the Bahá'í Community*. Los Angeles: Kalimát Press, 1987.

Cavalli-Sforza, Luigi Luca. *The Great Human Diaspora*. Reading, Mass.: Addison-Wesley Publishing, 1995.

Cavalli-Sforza, Luigi Luca, Paolo Menozzi, and Alberto Oiazza. *The History and Geography of Human Genes*. Princeton, N.J.: Princeton University Press, 1994.

Chopra, Deepak. *Quantum Healing*. New York: Bantam, 1989.

Collins, Chuck, Betty Leondar-Wright, and Holly Sklar. *Shifting Fortunes: The Perils of the Growing American Wealth Gap*. Boston: United for a Fair Economy, 1999.

Comas, J. *The Race Question in Modern Science*. Paris: UNESCO, 1958.

Conrad, Earl. *The Invention of the Negro*. New York: Paul S. Erickson, Inc., 1966.

Covey, Stephen R. *The Seven Habits of Highly Effective People: Restoring the Character Ethic*. New York: Simon and Schuster, 1989.

Dalai Lama [His Holiness Tenzin Gyatso the Fourteenth]. *Human Approach to World Peace*. London: Wisdom Publications, 1984.

Davenport, Francis Gardner, ed. *European Treaties Bearing on the History of the United States and Its Dependencies*. Washington, D.C.: Carnegie Institution of Washington Publications, 1917–1937.

Davis, Elizabeth Gould. *The First Sex*. New York: Penguin Books, 1971.

Davis, F. James. *Who Is Black?* University Park, Penn.: Pennsylvania State University Press, 1996.

Dobzhansky, Theodosius. "Eugenics in New Guinea," *Science* 132 (1960): 75–77.

Driver, Harold E. *Indians of North America*. 2d ed. Chicago: University of Chicago Press, 1969.

Eisler, Riane. *The Chalice and the Blade*. San Francisco: Harper and Row, 1987.

Erickson, Eric. *Life History and the Historical Moment*. New York: W. W. Norton, 1975.

Fishberg, M. *The Jews—A Study of Race and Environment*. London: Walter Scott Publishing, 1911.

Fishell, Leslie H., Jr., and Benjamin Quarels. *The Black American: A Documentary History*. Glenview, Ill.: Scott, Foresman and Company, 1967.

Foner, Philip S., ed. *Selections from the Writings of Frederick Douglass*. International Publishers, 1968.

Franklin, John Hope. *From Slavery to Freedom: A history of American Negroes*. New York: Alfred A. Knopf, 1967.

Frazer, Steven, ed. *The Bell Curve Wars*. New York: Basic Books, 1995.

Gandhi, Sunita, ed. *Qualities of Greatness: Selections from the World's Religions*. Washington, D.C.: The Council for Global Education, 1997.

de Gobineau, Count Arthur. *The Inequality of the Human Races*. Vol. 1. Translated by Adrian Collins. London: William Heinmann, 1915.

Goodman, Nathan G., ed. *A Benjamin Franklin Reader*. New York: Thomas Y. Crowell, 1945.

Gould, Stephen Jay. *The Mismeasure of Man*. New York: Norton, 1981.

Griffiths, Anthony J. F., and David T. Suzuki. *An Introduction to Genetic Analysis.* 5th ed. San Francisco: W. H. Freeman and Company, 1993.

Guzman, Pedro Miguel. *Medical Practices in Ancient America.* Mexico City: Ediciones Euroamericanas, 1985.

Hacker, Andrew. *Two Nations: Black and White, Separate, Hostile and Unequal.* New York: MacMillan, 1992.

Hakim, Joy. *US: An Age of Extremes.* New York: Oxford University Press, 1995.

Haller, John S. *Outcasts of Evolution: Scientific Attitudes of Racial Inferiority.* Carbondale, Ill.: Southern Illinois University Press, 1995.

Harris, Harry. *The Principles of Human Biochemical Genetics.* Amsterdam: North Holland Publishing; New York: American Elsevier, 1975.

Hughes, Thomas A. *The History of the Society of Jesus in North America: Colonial and Federal.* London: Longman and Green, 1910.

Hyman, Mark. *Blacks Before America.* Trenton, N.J.: Africa World Press, 1994.

Keyes, Ken, Jr. *The Hundreth Monkey.* Coos Bay, Ore.: Vision Books, 1981.

Khan, Janet A., and Peter J. Khan. *Advancement of Women: A Bahá'í Perspective.* Wilmette, Ill.: Bahá'í Publishing Trust, 1998.

King, James. *The Biology of Race.* Berkeley, Cal.: The University of California Press, 1981.

Koch, Adrienne, and William Peden, eds. *The Life and Selected Writings of Thomas Jefferson,* New York: Modern Library, 1944.

Koestler, Arthur. *The Thirteenth Tribe.* New York: Random House, 1976.

Kotulak, Ronald. "Learning How to Use the Brain," a paper delivered at the "Brain Development in Young Children: New Frontiers for Research, Policy and Practice" conference, Chicago, June 13, 1996.

Leakey, Richard E., and Roger Lewin. *Origins: What New Discoveries Reveal About the Emergence of Our Species and Its Possible Future.* New York: Dutton, 1977.

Lewontin, Richard C. *Human Diversity.* New York: Scientific American Library: [distributed by] W. H. Freeman, 1982.

———. *The Genetic Basis of Evolutionary Change.* New York: Columbia University Press, 1974.

———, Steven Rose, and Leon J. Kamin. *Not in Our Genes.* New York: Pantheon Books, 1984.

Lincoln, Eric C. *Religion and the Continuing American Dilemma.* New York: Hill and Wang, 1984.

Lipset, Seymour Martin. *American Exceptionalism: A Double-Edged Sword.* New York: W. W. Norton and Company, 1996.

Locke, Alain, and Benjamin Stern, eds. *When People Meet.* New York: Progressive Education Association, 1942.

Loewen, James W. *Lies My Teacher Told Me.* New York: The New Press, 1995.

Marius, Richard. *Luther.* Philadelphia: J. B. Lippincott and Company, 1974.

Martin, Waldo E., Jr. *The Mind of Frederick Douglass.* Chapel Hill, N.C.: University of North Carolina Press, 1984.

Mason, Philip. *Common Sense About Race.* New York: MacMillan Company, 1961.

Mazel, Ella. "And Don't Call Me a Racist," Boston: Argomount Press, 1998.

Montagu, Ashley. *Man's Most Dangerous Myth: The Fallacy of Race.* 4th ed. Cleveland: World Publishing, 1964.

Montagu, Ashley. *Most Dangerous Myth: The Fallacy of Race.*6th ed. Walnut Creek, Cal.: Altamira Press, 1997.

Moss, Jeffrey. *Oneness: Great Principles Shared by All Religions.* New York: Fawcett Columbine, 1989.

Murchie, Guy. *The Seven Mysteries of Life: An Exploration in Science and Philosophy.* Boston: Houghton Mifflin, 1978.

Pagels, Elaine. *Gnostic Gospels.* New York: Random House, 1979.

Popkin, Richard. *The High Road to Pyrrkonism.* San Diego: Austin Hill Press, 1980.

Rousseau, Jean-Jacques. *The Social Contract.* Translated by Judith R. Masters. Edited by Roger D. Masters. New York: St. Martin's Press, 1964.

Russell, Peter. *The Global Brain.* Los Angeles: J. T. Tarcher, Inc., 1983.

Rutstein, Nathan. *Racism: Unraveling the Fear.* Washington, D.C.: Global Classroom, 1997.

———. *Healing Racism in America: A Prescription for the Disease.* Springfield, Mass.: Whitcomb Publishers, 1993

———. *A Way Out of the Trap.* Springfield, Mass.: Whitcomb Publishers, 1995.

———, and Michael Morgan, eds. *Healing Racism: Education's Role.* Springfield, Mass.: Whitcomb Publishers, 1996.

Scholl, Steven, ed. *The Peace Bible: Words from the Great Traditions.* Los Angeles: Kalimát Press, 1986.

Smith, William, ed. *The Power of Race Unity.* Boston: Regional Council of the Bahá'ís of the Northeastern States, 1998.

Starr, Rita, ed. *Understanding the Cycle of Racial Conditioning—Unity in Diversity.* Evanston, Ill.: Healing Racism, Inc., 1996.

Steinem, Gloria. "What It Would Be Like If Women Win," in Diana L. Reische, ed. *Women and Society.* Wilson Co., 1972.

Takaki, Ronald. *A Different Mirror: A History of Multicultural America.* Boston: Little, Brown and Company, 1993.

Teilhard de Chardin, Pierre. *The Future of Man.* Translated from French by Norman Denny. New York: Harper and Row, 1964.

Thich Nhat Hanh. *Being Peace.* Berkeley, Cal.: Parallax Press, 1996.

Thomas, Richard. *Race Unity: An Imperative for Social Progress.* Ottawa, Ont.: Bahá'í Studies Publications, 1993.

Toynbee, Arnold J. *The Study of History.* Vol. 8. London: Oxford University Press, 1972.

Ueland, Brenda. *Strength to Your Sword Arm.* Duluth: Holy Cow Press, 1993.

van Sertima, Ivan. *They Came Before Columbus.* New York: Random House, 1976.

Walvin, James A. *The Black Presence: A Documentary History of the Negro in England, 1550–1860.* New York: Shocken Books, 1971.

Weatherford, Jack. *Indian Givers*. New York: Ballantine Books, 1988.

———. *Native Roots*. New York: Crown Publishing, 1991.

White, Leslie A. *The Science of Culture*. New York: Farrar and Strauss and Company, 1949.

Williamson, James A. *The Cabot Voyagers and Bristol Discovery Under Henry VII*. Cambridge, U.K.: Hakluyt Society, 1962.

Williamson, Joel. *A Rage for Order: Black/White Relations in the American South since Emancipation*. New York: Oxford University Press, 1986.

Wissler, Clark, Wilton M. Krogman, and Walter Krickerberg. *Medicine Among the American Indians*. [n. p.]: Acoma, 1939.

Zinn, Howard. *A People's History of the United States*. New York: Harper Perennial, 1980.